Inside the A

D0715456

ATHENIAN DEMOCRACY

INSIDE THE ANCIENT WORLD
General Editor: Michael Gunningham

The following titles are available in this series:

*Denotes books which are especially suited to GCSE or studies at a comparable 16+ level. The remainder may be useful at that level, but can also be used by students on more advanced courses.

Inside the Ancient World

ATHENIAN DEMOCRACY

Robin Barrow

BRISTOL CLASSICAL PRESS
General Editor: Michael Gunningham

for Paul

This Impression 2002

Previously published in Great Britain by
Macmillan Education Ltd, 1973
Thomas Nelson and Sons Ltd, 1992

Revised edition published in 1999 by
Bristol Classical Press
an imprint of
Gerald Duckworth & Co. Ltd
61 Frith Street
London W1V 5TA

Reprinted 1999

A catalogue record for this book is available
from the British Library

ISBN 1-85399-576-2

Printed in Great Britain by
Antony Rowe Ltd

Contents

Foreword to First Edition

To get *inside* the Ancient World is no easy task. What is easy is to idealise the Greeks and Romans, or else unconsciously to endow them with our own conventional beliefs and prejudices. The aim of this series is to illuminate selected aspects of Antiquity in such a way as to encourage the reader to form his own judgement, from the inside, on the ways of life, culture and attitudes that characterised the Greco-Roman world. Where suitable, the books draw widely on the writings (freshly translated) of ancient authors in order to convey information and to illustrate contemporary views.

The topics in the series have been chosen both for their intrinsic interest and because of their central importance for the student who wishes to see the civilisations of Greece and Rome in perspective. The close interaction of literature, art, thought and institutions reveals the Ancient World in its totality. The opportunity should thus arise for making comparisons not only within that world, between Athens and Sparta, or Athens and Rome, but also between the world of Antiquity and our own.

The title 'Classical Studies' (or 'Classical Civilisation') is featuring more and more frequently in school timetables and in the prospectuses of universities. In schools, the subject is now taught at Advanced Level as well as at Key Stages 3 and 4. It is particularly for the latter courses that this new series has been designed; also, as a helpful ancillary to the study of Greek and Latin in the sixth form and below. It is hoped that this book, and some others in the series, will interest students of History and English at these levels as well as the non-specialist reader.

The authors, who are teachers in schools or universities, have each taken an aspect of the Ancient World. They have tried not to give a romanticised picture but to portray, as vividly as possible, the Greeks and the Romans as they really were.

The primary aim of this book is to bring Athenian democracy to life. To this end Dr Barrow draws extensively on original sources, in particular on the Comedies of Aristophanes and the rich supply of examples that they furnish of the people of Athens, warts and all. The author traces the course of the democracy from its birth to its temporary death at the end of the fifth century, and suggests that in practice it was not always the Glory that some would have us believe. The Boule, the Ecclesia and the Law-courts, as well as the dominating figure of Pericles, are, as one might expect, brought before our gaze; but so are the demagogues and the informers. Women, slaves and ordinary citizens are not forgotten.

Throughout his survey Robin Barrow seeks to relate Athenian practice to our own, while at the same time maintaining an awareness of the important differences between the two civilisations. What kind of democracy, then, *was* Athens? That is one of the questions that this book tries to answer.

January 1973   MICHAEL GUNNINGHAM

Acknowledgements

The publishers wish to acknowledge the following sources of photographs:

American School of Classical Studies in Athens Figs 7, 13, 30, 36, 44; Trustees of the British Museum Figs 21, 22, 37, 38; J.M. Dent & Sons Ltd Fig 3; The Mansell Collection Figs 1, 2, 14, 18, 19, 20, 26, 27, 29, 32, 34, 40, 46; Metropolitan Museum of Art, New York Figs 16, 28; Musée Nationale, Louvre, Paris Fig 25; Royal Ontario Museum, Toronto, Ontario, Canada Fig 5; R. Sheridan Figs 4, 12, 35, 42, 47, 48; Vatican Fig 31; Wadsworth Atheneum, Hartford, Conn. Fig 41; Mrs D. Watson Fig 23.

The publishers have made every effort to contact the copyright holders. In cases where formal acknowledgement is not made, they will be pleased to make the necessary arrangements at the first opportunity.

List of Illustrations, Maps and Diagrams

Author's Note

In preparing this completely new edition of *Athenian Democracy* I have drawn on advice and criticism from a number of colleagues, and should like particularly to record my long-standing debt to Michael Gunningham, John Roberts and John Sharwood Smith.

One notable change of emphasis from previous editions is the overt reminder in the text to readers that evidence from ancient sources, particularly comic sources, cannot necessarily be taken at face value and should never be taken uncritically. Responsibility for this lies primarily with a certain Mr. Trappes-Lomax, who for many years has been fulminating against what he saw as my uncritical reliance on Aristophanes. Reading between the lines, I believe that Mr. Trappes-Lomax also takes exception to my unwillingness to endorse Athenian democracy as quite beyond reproach. Be that as it may, I have endeavoured in this edition to make it clear that while (as I should have thought hardly needs saying) ancient sources have to be interpreted and critically evaluated, and while the emergence of democracy in classical Athens was and remains an inspiration to us all, it was not without serious flaws, and the fact that virtually all our extant sources voice criticism of one kind or another is a fact not to be ignored nor uncritically dismissed as the bias of the bourgeoisie.

A word should be said about the translations. In no place, I hope, could they be described as inaccurate or distorted, but I have allowed myself a certain amount of freedom, particularly with Aristophanes, in order that a point intended by the author may be more clearly brought across to the modern reader. Two examples should suffice to illustrate this. A literal translation of *Ecclesiazusae*, line 133, might run: 'Why have I put on this garland?' The situation in the play at this point makes use of the fact that a garland was worn both by the speaker at an Assembly and at drinking parties. In order to make the point clear to the modern reader, unfamiliar with the associative ideas of the Athenians, I have added the following: 'I thought that this wreath was the sort of thing worn at drinking parties' (see p. 48). Similarly, in order to convey clearly the rather complicated story of Alcibiades' trick played on the Spartan ambassadors (p. 46), I have conflated the two accounts of the incident given by Plutarch in his lives of Nicias and of Alcibiades. The intention of the original has at all times been treated as more important than the vocabulary, the spirit more important than the grammar. But, as I say, there is no conscious mistranslation.

1
Introduction

Democracy

Today, in many parts of the world, we tend to take 'democracy' for granted. We are perhaps inclined to assume that it is obviously the best form of government. It took the ancient world quite a long time to come round to this point of view. But when democracy first arose, in the city (*polis*) of Athens,

1. *Reconstruction of the Acropolis*

it was, in some respects, a far more extreme type of democracy than the modern world has produced. This is partly because, at least before recent developments in telecommunications, the size of most countries today makes it difficult if not impossible for us to decide every political issue by a direct vote of the people. For that and other reasons, typically, now we elect representatives, members of parliament and so on, and leave the decision-making to them, merely reserving the right to vote against them at the next election if we don't like what they have done.

During the fifth century BC the *polis* of Athens had about 50,000 citizens. Attica, the area in which they lived, is roughly 1000 square miles. It was a practical possibility for such a small number of people to debate and decide all matters at a public assembly (*Ecclesia*).

Of course it would not have worked very well if all 50,000 had been in the habit of turning up at the same time. The Pnyx, the sloping hill where the *Ecclesia* was held, would not have taken them all; but naturally, when one of

2. *The Pnyx*

the forty or so regular meetings of the year took place, some citizens would be ill, some too busy and some just too bored to attend. In parts of the world today, we only have to vote once every five years, and even so only about 75 per cent of the electorate bother to do so. For some citizens attendance at the *Ecclesia* would involve a journey of some miles, perhaps on foot, and the elderly, at least, may well have been discouraged from attending by this sort of consideration. For one reason or another, then, enough people would choose not to go to make it possible for those who did to be present and to take a direct part in the politics of the day.

The Council (*Boule*) would have previously drawn up an agenda of the things to be discussed by the *Ecclesia*, and we may be sure that there will have been some prominent people, well known for their political activity in the past, who will have taken a lead in the debate and have had some following amongst the people. But everybody – no matter who he was – had the right to speak, and no decision could be taken which did not meet with the approval of the majority of those present. In this way it was literally true that the people ruled, and this is what the word 'democracy' means in the original Greek: the people (*demos*) rule (*kratei*).

The Assembly in action

In the *Acharnians*, a comedy written towards the end of the fifth century, Aristophanes gives us a picture of the Assembly in action. Dicaiopolis, the

3. *The Agora*

hero, whose name means 'good city', is a poor farmer whose livelihood has been ruined by the war that Athens was then waging with Sparta. Sparta and her allies march up into Attica during the summer months and burn all the crops, while the Athenians take refuge within the city walls. For Dicaiopolis the situation is intolerable. What is he getting out of the war? Nothing. What is he losing? Everything. He has decided that peace must be made with the enemy, so he has come into the city early in the morning to get a front place at the *Ecclesia*, obviously because he is afraid that he won't get a proper hearing if several thousand people come and he is stuck at the back.

From his position on the still deserted Pnyx, Dicaiopolis can see down into the market place (*agora*), which was much more than a mere place for buying and selling. The *agora* was the centre of the *polis*' activity. Because of the good climate and their agricultural background, the Athenians were an open-air, sociable people, and it was here, in the place to which all the main roads led, that they would meet; here also that most of the main public buildings such as the council chamber were built. Above the *agora* rose the

3

Acropolis ('the high-spot of the city'). All Greek cities had originally been situated on hills for defensive reasons, but as the size of the city increased its *akropolis* became too small to offer protection even in time of trouble; and so what had originally been the citadel itself became instead the symbolic centre of the city. On the Acropolis at Athens, for instance, was built a great temple to the city's Goddess Athene (the Parthenon). Finally, if Dicaiopolis turns his head in the other direction he can see out over the countryside of Attica.

4. *A view of the Acropolis from the Pnyx*

At the moment he is in an extremely bad mood.

DICAIOPOLIS: Everything's wrong. Has anything good happened? Well, I suppose if I thought hard enough I could think of about four things – compared with an ocean of disasters... Just look: we have an assembly called for this morning, and who is there here? Absolutely nobody. Where are they? Chattering about in the *agora*, trying to avoid coming. No sense of responsibility. Not even the councillors on duty have come and they're supposed to conduct it. Oh but they'll come; only they'll come late, pushing and shoving each other trying to get through to a place at the front. But they're not interested in making peace. Heavens, no. Oh, city, my city. I'm always first here and I sit alone yawning and fidgeting, pulling my hair out, gazing lovingly away from the city towards the countryside and longing for peace – and to get away from the sordid money-grubbing city. Well, here I am anyway. Ready to shout and interrupt if ever they talk about anything except peace. Ah, here they are: the councillors, late sleepers all of them, shoving their way through to the front, just like I said.

The councillors take their place at the front and a herald addresses the *Ecclesia* with the traditional question: 'Who wishes to address the Assembly?'

> A CITIZEN: I do.
> HERALD: Who are you?
> CITIZEN: Amphitheus, or Godish to you.
> HERALD: Godish? aren't you a man?
> CITIZEN: No; I'm an immortal. My great great great greatly squared great ancestor was the goddess Demeter. So I'm immortal; and it is the will of the Gods that I should be entrusted with the task of making peace with Sparta. But although I'm immortal I haven't enough money to get to Sparta, and these councillors won't give me any.
> HERALD: That's enough criticism from you; throw him out.
> CITIZEN: Help, help.
> DICAIOPOLIS: Councillors, please. This is most irregular, dragging away a man who only wants to get us peace and an end to this war.
> [Aristophanes, *Acharnians* 1 ff.]

Further interruptions occur before Dicaiopolis realises that his fellow citizens are not going to agree with his point of view, and so he makes a private peace with the enemy.

We must not, incidentally, take Aristophanes too literally, and his plays as a whole cannot be used uncritically as direct evidence for Athenian thought or practice. He is a writer of comedies, and the idea of one citizen making a private peace in this instance is of course a joke. Nonetheless, Athenian comedy, like satire as disparate as that of W.S. Gilbert, *Private Eye*, *Saturday Night Live* or *Spitting Image*, is always very topical. If Aristophanes writes a play about abuses of the jury system, or political demagogues, we may be sure that these phenomena are familiar to his audience; if the joke is that women take an active part in politics we may reasonably infer that in truth women played no such part. More generally, Aristophanes himself would seem, on the evidence of his plays, to have disliked the war between Athens and Sparta and their allies that took place during the last quarter of the fifth century, and to have felt that there was something to criticise in the actual practice of the democracy. In the following pages a number of scenes from Aristophanes' plays will be quoted, and it is perhaps necessary to stress that I do this in full recognition of the care that needs to be exercised. One does not take a comic writer, a satirist, at face value; one does not, generally, quote him as the evidence, but one does turn to him for illustration (however distorted for comic effect), for implication and suggestion. In addition most of Aristophanes' plays are full of references, generally insulting, to contemporary people and events. In this play, for instance, the plot itself, the idea of making peace, is clearly related to the harsh fact that Athens was indeed then at war; and although the scene just quoted is pure fiction taken as a whole, the procedural

5. *Restoration of the Acropolis as it would have been in Dicaiopolis' day*

details, such as the herald's call for speakers and the open response of an unknown citizen, presumably provide a realistic picture of the sort of thing that might take place in the *Ecclesia*, where all citizens of any sort might meet and freely put their point of view.

It had not always been so.

2
The Emergence of Democracy

Aristocratic society

Four hundred years before the time of Dicaiopolis, eighth-century Greece
had been an aristocratic society. A man owed his loyalty to one of the noble
families: if the head of that family was going to war he would expect to lead
out a contingent of all the peasants who lived scattered about on his land. In
time of peace the peasants would be grateful if he did not make too many
demands on them. The nobles made the decisions and gave the orders; the
mass of the people simply obeyed them.

We get some idea of the enormous division between the two classes
in the scene in Homer's *Iliad* where Agamemnon, the leader of the united
Greek forces, orders an Assembly. This was an Assembly very different from
the one that Dicaiopolis was to attend so many years later. The ordinary
soldiers are present, but they are not supposed to speak: they are there to listen
to the nobles, their betters. However on this occasion a commoner, named
Thersites, does dare to speak – with sad consequences for himself:

> All the rest sat down and kept their places except Thersites who
> went babbling on. He was ugly, bow-legged and crippled: he had
> round shoulders and an ill-shaven warped head. In a shrill bleating
> voice he began to criticise Agamemnon, much to the annoyance
> of the rest of the Greeks...and when he had finished, the noble
> Odysseus approached him in fury and said angrily: 'Thersites, you
> intolerable creature...don't start trying to quarrel with kings,
> you, the most inferior low-born wretch among the Greeks...if I catch
> you making a fool of yourself like this again, I'll lay hold of you,
> strip you naked and beat you black and blue till you run howling
> back to the ships.' When he had said this Odysseus took his stick
> and beat the man on the back until he fell down in a huddle with
> great bloody bruises on his shoulders and a tear in his eye.

To really understand aristocratic society, in which everyone has his place
and must keep it, it is necessary to read on and to note the reaction of the

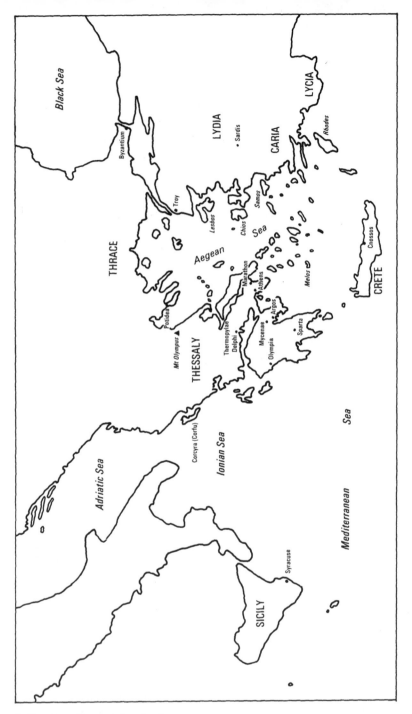

6. *Greece and surrounding lands*

Greeks, including Thersites' fellow-soldiers. They do not resent Odysseus' behaviour. On the contrary:

> They laughed cheerfully and murmured to each other: 'Certainly Odysseus has done countless great things in the past, both in battle and in debate, but without doubt teaching this disgraceful babbler a lesson is the best thing that he's done to date'.
>
> [Homer, *Iliad* 2.211 ff.]

The Homeric poems were themselves probably designed for an aristocratic audience, so we cannot reasonably infer from this passage that the common people in fact accepted rule by the nobles without resentment. But the *Iliad* certainly suggests, what is not that uncommon, a society in which different classes take it for granted in practical terms that they have different fates allotted to them, different roles to play. So everybody jeers at Thersites and feels he get no more than his due, because it was not his place, as a common peasant, to criticise the better people. We may doubt whether, if the nobles had always behaved as brutally as this, the people would have endured the situation for long. Yet although this sort of scene might rarely have taken place, the people (*demos*) in the early days of Greek aristocratic society were effectively slaves of the nobles, and for some time they accepted this state of affairs without overt objection.

By 700 BC, however, complaints were beginning to be made. A Boeotian farmer, Hesiod, wrote a poem in which he blamed the nobles and their greed for the hardships of the common people:

> Don't you realise, you nobles, that justice will one day be done? For the Gods are watching over us always, and they can see when one of you takes unfair advantage of other men, ruining them completely and not giving a damn about what the Gods think... Justice sees, and Justice carries this message to the Gods: the mass of common people have to pay for your greed and wickedness.

Hesiod knows well enough why the 'money-eating' nobles are able to get away with their injustice: they have the power. He makes this point in a fable, in which a hawk represents the nobles and a nightingale the helpless *demos*:

> A hawk seized a nightingale in its claws and flew high into the clouds with its victim cruelly hooked beneath it. And when the nightingale cried out in its misery, the hawk said roughly: 'What are you screaming about? I'm the boss and you'll have to go where I

9

take you, however much you scream. I could let you go. I could eat you. What I do depends on what I feel like. I'm the stronger of us two, and only a fool would try to fight against somebody stronger.'

[Hesiod, *Works and Days* 203 ff.]

The breakdown of aristocratic society

During the next two centuries the situation changed. Trading and colonisation upset the firm and unquestioned leadership of the nobles, because they provided ways in which the peasant farmers could escape from the farmland on which they had been born. Knowledge of foreign customs and different ways of life, which will have reached the ears of everybody through traders, will also have encouraged people to question the right of the nobles to give all the orders; and some who became rich through trading will have presented a direct challenge to the superiority of the landowning aristocracy. A society which is based on the quiet acceptance of traditional customs, like ancient aristocratic society or a primitive tribal society today, can never remain the same once it has frequent contact with societies of a different kind.

There was another rather curious reason for the weakening of the nobles' supremacy: in the past, battles had been lost or won by the fighting of individual warriors. The noble, as well as regarding himself as superior at home in time of peace, was expected to show himself superior on the field of battle. Men like Odysseus and Achilles did something to earn their right to leadership by their hand-to-hand fighting against Trojan heroes such as Hector. But now a new battle formation was adopted: soldiers (*hoplites*) formed together in a rectangle, each man interlocking and covering his neighbour with his shield, and battles were won or lost by the combined efforts of the hoplites. There was no longer an opportunity for individuals to earn fame and gratitude from their followers in war. To be a hoplite one had to be able to afford the necessary armour, so that a new middle class of hoplites arose. Since it was on the hoplite class that the safety of all now depended, it was natural that it should challenge the right of the nobles to rule.

As a result of these changes the nobles began to lose their authority throughout the Greek world. People began to identify themselves with a place rather than with some noble, and so the idea of a city came into being, now with three groups of people to be considered: the nobles, the middle class of hoplites, and the poor. A time of upheaval followed, and in most cities tyrants managed to set themselves up in power. But it is to Athens that we must now confine our attention.

Solon and Athens

In 600 BC the noble families still held all the real power in Athens. The government consisted of nine magistrates, known as *archons,* who were chosen annually on consideration of their birth and wealth, and the council of the *Areopagus,* which was made up of all the ex-archons and which sat as a court of justice in all matters. In theory the nobles had it all sewn up in their favour, but as the Aristotelian *Constitution of Athens* tells us:

> There had been tension and enmity for a long time between the nobles and the common people, because politically speaking the government was an *oligarchy* ['rule-by-the-few'], and especially because the poor and their families were slaves of the rich. The few, that is to say the nobles, possessed all the land and if the poor failed to pay a rent they could be sold into slavery. A man had to give his own person as security for a debt, until Solon first became leader of the people. The thing that the many (the common people) found most intolerable was the fact that they were bound as serfs to the nobles; but they were also dissatisfied in every other way too, since they had no share in anything...and so the many finally rose up against the few. And when *stasis* (civil war) had become violent, both sides, in agreement, chose Solon to mediate between them.
> [Aristotle, *Constitution of Athens* 2 ff. The *Constitution of Athens* is traditionally ascribed to Aristotle, but generally not thought to be his work. It also has to be used with care as evidence for the 5th century, particularly the second half beginning at Section 42.]

The picture has certain points in common with a modern industrial dispute: two opposing and irreconcilable sides, and the appointment of an arbitrator. Solon was well suited to play the middle man, for, although aristocratic by birth, he was not a landowner but a trader. He became *archon* in 594 BC, and the first thing he did was to put an end to the possibility of one Athenian being enslaved to another as the result of debt. He then proceeded to reorganise the political arrangements and it is here that we find the basis of the future democracy.

He divided the people into four classes based on wealth, thus taking account of those who had made their money by trading and, theoretically, putting an end to the privileges of those who were simply well born. The richest class, the *pentacosiomedimni* (those whose property produced 500 measures of corn, olive oil or wine – a considerable amount), were alone to be eligible for the archonships, which were still the most important offices in the state; lesser magistracies would be open to the second and third classes as well, the *knights* and *zeugites*. The lowest, and by far the largest class, the *thetes,* were to be entitled only to attend the Assembly and the law-courts (Fig. 8).

The right to attend the Assembly was not in itself very much. There had been, as we have seen, an Assembly of sorts even in the aristocratic society

7. *Official Measures*

of the past; the question is obviously what powers Solon gave to the Assembly, and it seems fairly clear that the answer is very few. Yet it was a step towards the ultimate power of the Assembly, for now at least it was written down that all citizens, however poor, had the right to attend the *Ecclesia*. In the same way, whatever Solon actually intended to achieve by allowing even *thetes* to play a part in the law-courts, we do know that this

Name of Class	Income Qualification	Political Rights	Military Role
1. PENTACOSIO-MEDIMNI	500 measures of corn, oil or wine	Membership of Areopagus; Archonship; other public offices	
2. KNIGHTS	300 measures	Public office other than Archonship	Serving in cavalry
3. ZEUGITES	200 measures	Public office other than Archonship	Serving as hoplites
4. THETES	Anything less than 200	Attendance at Assembly and as jurors in law-courts	Light infantry or sailors

8. *The classes in Attica after Solon*

right was later to become a most important feature of the full democracy. For when the people control the courts, when it is the people who judge and condemn, it is very much harder for the rulers to get away with sharp practice. This is one of the reasons why in England there is a long-standing tradition that the law-courts, the judiciary as it is called, should be more or less separate from government. The situation was very different in Rome during the last years of the Republic: there the courts, when in the hands of the nobility, served almost as a protection for a criminal provincial governor. He could

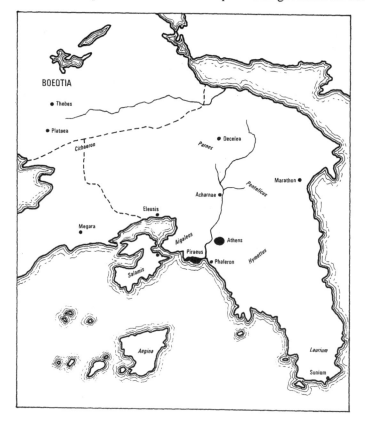

9. *Map of Attica*

steal or plunder more or less what he liked, safe in the knowledge that he would be tried by a number of his fellows, who would have no interest in convicting him for something that they themselves would hope to do – should they become governors of some rich province.

Solon did not create Athenian democracy; nobody did. It arose gradually. But he had laid the foundation for it. He broke the traditional pattern of superiority being dependent on birth; he put an end to the enslavement of fellow citizens; he established by law that all citizens had some rights; and to the poorest he gave rights that were later to be extremely important to them. He was not on anybody's side, but was concerned to stabilise a revolutionary situation and to give something to everybody. Unfortunately, nobody was satisfied. The landed nobles were annoyed because they had lost their firm control and superiority, and the poor because they did not think that they had been given enough. When Solon left Athens to travel the world, the city was once again thrown into confusion.

Cleisthenes' reforms (c. 507 BC)

Some time after Solon, order was restored in the city by Peisistratus, who set himself up as tyrant. He was succeeded by his sons Hippias and Hipparchus, and when Hipparchus was murdered, Hippias, through fear, became a harsh and unpopular ruler. The resentment that was felt against him was too good an opportunity for one important noble family to miss. This was the Alcmaeonid family, who had been expelled from Athens by Peisistratus, presumably because they had opposed him and had been too powerful to be ignored. They now returned with the help of a Spartan army and drove Hippias out.

The man who emerged as the leader of the Alcmaeonids was Cleisthenes and he now proceeded to give the Athenian constitution a further overhaul but not, as might be expected, in the interests of the nobles. On the contrary, building on Solon's work, Cleisthenes went even further in the same direction and his political arrangements were to form the central part of the democratic system which developed rapidly after his death.

Cleisthenes' changes went deep and must have upset many a person with traditional views. As far back as any Athenian could remember the population had been divided into four tribes, each one tracing its ancestry to some legendary founder.

A tribe consisted of various *phratries,* which were something like Scottish clans. Each of these *phratries* was made up of several families, using that word in its widest sense (*genos*). Each *genos* in turn consisted of a number of *oikoi* (families, in the narrow sense of the word) (Fig. 10). The structure of each tribe thus resembled a pyramid, all the members of which were theoretically related. No doubt, as the population grew, the significance of the arrangement would grow less. In a population of, say, 30,000 families it is unlikely that one would automatically feel any identity with a stranger who happened to come from the same tribe, especially when the increasing mobility of people over the years will have meant that one might live miles away from other members of one's tribe. Nevertheless Cleisthenes must have caused some dismay when he 'redistributed the whole population into ten new tribes, with the aim,' says Aristotle, 'of mixing up the people so that a

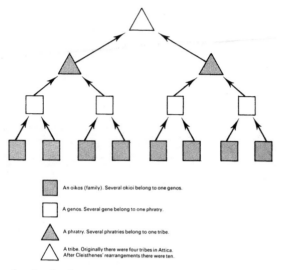

An oikos (family). Several okioi belong to one genos.

A genos. Several gene belong to one phratry.

A phratry. Several phratries belong to one tribe.

A tribe. Originally there were four tribes in Attica.
After Cleisthenes' rearrangements there were ten.

10. *Diagram showing family groups*

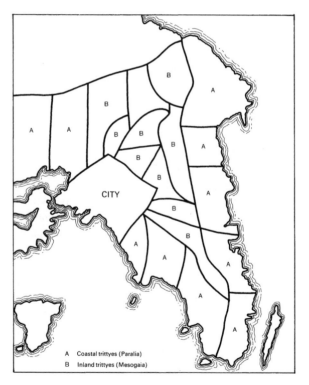

A   Coastal trittyes (Paralia)
B   Inland trittyes (Mesogaia)

11. *Cleisthenes' division of Attica*

greater number could share in political administration', for, of course, these ten new tribes were artificially created and did not pretend to be blood groups.

Cleisthenes divided Attica into thirty parts (*trittyes*), of which ten were areas of land near the coast, ten inland, and ten in the *polis* itself. Each tribe was to consist of three parts, one from each section. This meant that each tribe contained people of differing interests and ways of life: those living inland would tend to be farmers or herdsmen, those by the coast fishermen,

12. *Model of the Agora showing Tholos and council-house*

those in the city involved in some kind of industrial work. In addition, the apparently trivial decree that a man should now refer to himself, not as 'the son of so-and-so', but as coming 'from such-and-such a village (*deme*)' will have further broken down the old ties of family and blood. Solon's classification of the people into four economic classes was retained, and the archonship was still open only to the richest class (the *pentacosiomedimni*). Moreover, the *Areopagus* continued to be an influential body. Then Cleisthenes made two important innovations.

According to some authorities Solon had created a Council (*Boule*) to consist of 400 citizens; the evidence for this is not strong and nothing is known of any activity by such a *Boule*. Cleisthenes made a *Boule* of 500 citizens a central feature of his arrangements, either developing the Solonian Council or creating it out of nothing. Each of the ten new tribes was to elect by lot fifty members to represent it for a year at a time on the *Boule*. Any citizen over the age of thirty was eligible and, since no one was allowed to serve on it more than twice, any citizen might expect to serve on it during his lifetime. Each tribe's contingent of fifty took it in turn, for one tenth of the year, to take over the presidency (*prytaneia*) of the *Boule*, the members of the contingent being known as the *prytaneis* during that period of the year. Each day a different member of the contingent would be entrusted with the keys to the public buildings of the city and act as the supreme chairman (*epistates*). This is the Aristotelian account of the function of the *Boule* as it was in the middle of the fifth century:

> Those who are serving their turn as *prytaneis* dine together in the building known as the *Tholos* (where they also sleep during their presidency) at the public expense; they arrange meetings of the full *Boule* and the *demos* – the council meets every day, except public holidays, and the *demos* normally assembles four times during each *prytaneia*. The *prytaneis* give written notice beforehand of the business to be transacted by the *Boule*.
>
> [Aristotle, *Constitution of Athens* 43.3 ff.]

The *Boule* was thus a sort of miniature civil service (though with the very important difference from our own civil service that it did not consist of permanent officials), whose job was not to make policy so much as to ensure the smooth running of political matters; but the influence of the *prytaneis* in office at any given time could obviously be quite considerable, since they gave active leadership to the *Boule*, and, in concert with their colleagues, decided what would be discussed at the Assembly of the *demos* and acted as chairmen there. The *Boule* was also responsible for dealing with charges of treason.

In Aristophanes' comedy the *Knights* there is a parody of a Council meeting. The speaker, a sausage-seller, is destined to replace Paphlagon as the popular leader in the play, because he is even more abominable and unscrupulous in his flattery of the people than Paphlagon (who is meant to represent the politician Cleon, for whom Aristophanes had a particular loathing):

> SAUSAGE-SELLER: Listen, you'll like this story. I belted after Paphlagon and found him storming away before the *Boule*, pounding huge and ridiculous insults out against the Knights. It was quite clear to me, judging from their solemn faces and nodding heads, that the councillors were swallowing every lie he told.... I broke through the railings holding the spectators back, after muttering a prayer for the blessing of a quick tongue, and bellowed: 'Councilmen, good news. Good news indeed. Haddock is down in price for the first time since this war started.' Quick as a flash their solemn nodding stopped; they smiled with pleasure; this *was* good news, and they

voted me a garland as a reward for bringing such important news. But Paphlagon, being no fool, saw that I was merely distracting the attention of the *Boule* from listening to his charges, and knowing as well as anyone what sort of thing pleases the *Boule*, he tried to outbid me by saying 'Friends, I feel moved to offer one hundred oxen for sacrifice in view of this good news'. The Council immediately began to take note of him again. Not to be outdone I replied 'Two hundred oxen is my offer'. Heads were turned in my direction again...and so, to cut a long story short, the Council is now firmly in my pocket.

[Aristophanes, *Knights* 625 ff.]

13. *Ostraka: Aristeides, Themistocles, Cimon and Pericles. There is a story that a citizen, being unable to write himself, turned to his neighbour and asked him to inscribe the name of Aristeides for him. His neighbour obliged; it was none other than Aristeides himself*

Behind the absurdity of Aristophanes' exaggeration it is clear that the favour of the *Boule* was important in politics at Athens, though it should also be remembered that this play was written some seventy-five years after Cleisthenes had established the *Boule*. When first created, its influence will have been less.

The second novel feature of Cleisthenes' proposals was the introduction of ostracism. This was a device for getting rid of unwelcome public figures. If a minimum of six thousand citizens could be found who were willing to

18

inscribe the name of any politician on a piece of pottery (*ostrakon*) – which served the purpose of paper – that politician had to leave Attica for a period of ten years. This was preferable to a normal decree of exile, partly because it was legally established that the period of exile should last only ten years, and partly because during that period the man's property would not be expropriated by political enemies. In a sense, ostracism involved an enforced cooling-off period, rather than the ruin of political opponents.

We must not imagine that Cleisthenes, any more than Solon, created democracy. The archons were still the supreme magistrates, and they could only come from the wealthiest class; furthermore, the *Areopagus*, consisting of all the ex-archons, was still a very influential body. Though all citizens were allowed to attend the *Ecclesia* we do not know that it was yet very powerful, but at least the important framework of the future democracy had been laid down: the Assembly now had regular meetings; the people still had the law-courts in their hands; the *Boule*, which at some point during the fifth century became open to all citizens including *thetes* (though the poor may not have welcomed the chance to serve prior to the introduction of payment), was inevitably going to become increasingly important. Above all, the ancient loyalties of family and tribe, which had contributed greatly to the actual power of the noble families, had been broken. 'After the reforms of Cleisthenes', says Aristotle, 'the political structure became more democratic.' [Constitution of Athens 22.1] Clearly all that stood in the way of proper democracy, with political affairs in the hands of the *Ecclesia* and *Boule*, was the prestige and importance of the *archons* and the *Areopagus*. Between 500 and 460 BC these obstacles to the power of the people were removed.

The final steps to democracy

In 490 BC the Persians, under King Darius, crossed the Hellespont and marched down into Greece with a vast force, which, amazingly, was defeated by the Athenians (and the Plataeans) at the battle of Marathon. This victory was owed effectively to the Athenian *hoplites*, the middle or *zeugite* class, and almost certainly this clear example of their importance to the city had something to do with the weakening of the authority of the *pentacosiomedimni*. In the next ten years three prominent members of the aristocracy (two relatives of the ex-tyrant Hippias, and Megacles, a leading Alcmaeonid) were ostracised and, even more significant, in 487 the *archons* were chosen for the first time by lot and not by election. Although even now only members of the top two income groups could be *archons*, the fact that appointment depended on luck rather than management naturally made the office less attractive to aspiring politicians and hence less influential. Furthermore, the *Areopagus* was also bound to lose authority in time, since it would no longer consist of those who had actually been chosen to hold the highest office in the state.

The result was that the important political office now became the generalship (*strategia*); but the *strategoi* (generals), unlike the *archons* in the past, did not legally have to belong to any particular income group. Also they were elected by all the people, each tribe voting for one *strategos* to represent itself so that there were ten altogether. The *strategoi* were therefore the people's representatives in a way that the *archons* had never been.

14. *Warship and merchantman*

In 480, during a second invasion, the Persian fleet was crushingly defeated at the sea battle of Salamis, which, although nominally fought by the Greeks, was effectively won by the Athenians and Themistocles, one of their *strategoi*. But just as at Marathon the hoplites had proved themselves indispensable to the city, so at Salamis the lowest income group, the *thetes*, who formed the bulk of the rowers, made it clear that if Athens' future was to be based upon her sea power, then the thetic class was essential to that future.

Events were thus cementing the formal arrangements made by Cleisthenes. Every citizen could regard himself as essential to the security and fame of the *polis*; the most important office was dependent on a vote of all the people; necessarily the whole citizen body, and therefore the Assembly and *Boule*, became the real power of the state. The final dramatic stroke indicating the birth of this new power came in 462 when, during the absence of Cimon, the most prominent of the conservative aristocratic leaders, a man named Ephialtes pushed through a reform depriving the *Areopagus* (which despite recent events still had considerable prestige) of all its functions save jurisdiction over homicide, arson and the destruction of sacred olive trees.

In his play the *Persians*, which celebrates the Greek victory over Xerxes at Salamis, Aeschylus shows awareness of and enthusiasm for the momentous changes under way at Athens: the establishment of a free society of all citizens, who, in theory, would be held in check not by superiors but only by respect for the law. Atossa, the mother of the king, asks the chorus of Persian elders to tell her about this victorious city, Athens:

> ATOSSA: Tell me, in what part of the world is this Athens situated?
> CHORUS: Far away to the West where the sun sinks down.
> ATOSSA: But did my son wish to conquer a place so far away?
> CHORUS: Indeed he did; for were Athens but defeated, all Greece would fall before him.
> ATOSSA: Is the Athenian army so enormous then?
> CHORUS: So powerful is the Athenian army that it has caused havoc among the mighty host of our Persian army.
> ATOSSA: And are they a wealthy people as well?
> CHORUS: Their land produces silver.
> ATOSSA: Do they fight with a bow, as we do?
> CHORUS: Why, no; they fight hand-to-hand, with shield and spear.
> ATOSSA: And who is their Lord and Master?
> CHORUS: Madam, they are neither slaves nor servants to any man.
>
> [Aeschylus, *Persians* 231 ff.]

Several thousand hearts in the audience must have beaten a little faster with pride and satisfaction. Were they not Athenians? Had they not routed the vast hordes of Persia? Rich, strong, and slaves to no man. That was Athens. A democracy and proud of it.

15. *Spear versus bow*

3
Radical Democracy

Athenian achievements

The years from c. 462 BC to 431 BC (from the establishment of a radical democracy to the outbreak of the Peloponnesian war) were good years for Athens. Abroad, the alliance that she had made in 479 BC with the Ionian Greeks against the common enemy, Persia, became a mighty empire under

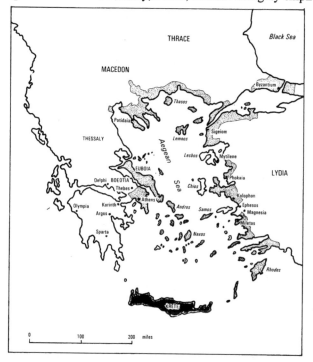

16. *Map showing extent of Athenian Empire about 450* BC

her domination. Tribute was paid to Athens annually by the member states, in return for which she built up and maintained a fleet of three hundred triremes which monopolised the Aegean, securing, amongst other things, trade routes for the import of corn and for the export of Athenian oil, wine and vases. The tribute was originally kept in the League treasury on the island of Delos (which was why the alliance of Ionians and Athenians was first known as the Delian League); but in 454 BC the Athenians moved the treasury to Athens itself, a sure sign that they were now giving the orders.

With money from surplus tribute and also from taxes levied on ships putting in to trade at the thriving market in the Peiraeus (the harbour a few miles from the city itself), a great new public building programme was

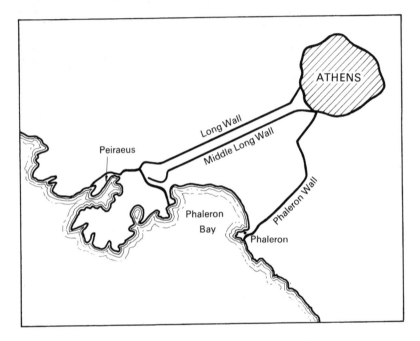

17. *Map showing Athens, Peiraeus and Phaleron Bay*

launched. On the Acropolis the Parthenon began to rise, a monument to the glory of the goddess Athene and the city itself. A new and imposing gateway (*Propylaia*) was built as well, through which all the state and religious processions leading to the Parthenon would enter following the path up the side of the Acropolis from the *agora* below.

These magnificent buildings did not rise without opposition. Enemies of Pericles, who was the man mainly responsible for the building programme, cried out in the Assembly

> that Athens had sacrificed her reputation by taking the tribute of the allies and using it in this way. The allies are going to be infuriated, they said. They are going to call this nothing less than tyranny when they see that, with the money they paid unwillingly as a contribution

18. *The Parthenon*

19. *The Propylaia*

to the defence against Persia, we are decorating our city and making it beautiful, like some conceited girl powdering her nose.

[Plutarch, *Pericles* 12 ff.]

Pericles replied that, provided Athens afforded protection for the allies against Persia with her navy, which she was doing and would continue to do, it was nobody's business but her own what she did with any money left over. He was also concerned that the unskilled citizens

should have a way of earning some of the national income, and yet that they should not simply be given a dole while doing nothing. And so he proposed to the Assembly his plans for buildings and other public works which would give employment to a lot of people, with a lot of different abilities, for a long time to come. Stone, bronze, ivory, gold, ebony and cypress wood would all be needed and so there would be work for carpenters, metalworkers, painters and so on, not to mention people to transport these materials; then there would be rope-makers, weavers, road-builders...

[Plutarch, *Pericles* 12 ff.]

Providing such employment was one method of giving every citizen a chance to earn a share of the enormous wealth of the city. But these buildings were not only built by the people; they were also for the people. In the same way a number of public festivals and sacrifices were held during the year, to the advantage of all the citizens, public baths and gymnasia were built, and eventually even seats in the theatre were subsidised by the state. The Old Oligarch explains:

The Athenian people are aware that it is impossible for a poor citizen on his own to offer sacrifices to the Gods, to provide enormous feasts, to set up religious shrines and so to contribute to the greatness and beauty of the city, but they have discovered a way round this problem. The city itself, at the expense of the whole people, holds sacrifices to the Gods and all the people take part in the public feasts. Some of the richer citizens have their own private baths and gymnasia, but the people as a whole have access to public baths and gymnasia with the result that the mass of ordinary people are in fact better off in this respect than the wealthy aristocrats.

[Old Oligarch, *Constitution of Athens* 2.9 ff.]

During these years, as Athenian power grew, there were other signs of her greatness: sculpture and vase painting flourished. Aeschylus, Sophocles and Euripides were all writing at some time during the period. And, perhaps most important of all, Athens became a centre for all manner of people who realised that here was a state in which they could be free to pursue whatever branch of learning interested them. Scientists, historians, philosophers, all were to be found at Athens. In particular a number of professional teachers of such things as skill in public debating found their way there. Generally referred to as the 'sophists' (wise men), although they were not in any true sense a group, they were in great demand amongst those who could afford their high fees, since the state itself provided nothing that we should call higher education.

20. *A Bronze mirror*   21. *Jewellery*

That great things were achieved, that a tremendous energy and confidence were released during these years cannot be denied; and the achievement must surely be attributed largely to the new freedom. Democracy meant that the people ruled and that meant that they were doing what they wanted to do, which, in turn, meant that they were enthusiastic. The point is well put by Herodotus, who, though not an Athenian, found his way there in the middle of the century. He makes the following comment in reference to the Athenian courage displayed against the Persians when the democracy was newly born:

> It is absolutely clear from thousands of examples that freedom is a prize well worth winning. Take the Athenians: in the past, when fighting under a tyrant, they showed themselves to be no more courageous than anyone else; but as soon as they got rid of their tyrant, then straightaway they became the most courageous people of all. What this shows is that when they were under the compulsion

of an overlord and felt that they were merely fighting for his sake they didn't mind if they were beaten in battle, because any victory would be *his* victory. But once they were free then each man was fighting for himself and determined to do the best he could.

[Herodotus, v 78 ff.]

Athenian pride

The Athenians were very conscious and proud of their city and its democracy, as we may see in this extract from a play by Euripides. Although the conventions of Athenian drama generally demanded that the stories should be set in the mythical past, and therefore that the states had to be shown as being ruled by kings, this does not prevent Euripides praising the qualities of the democratic Athens he knew, as if they had existed in the past. In this scene a herald arrives at Athens from Thebes and, naturally enough, asks for the king:

HERALD: Who is the king of this land? To whom should I give my message from Creon, king of Thebes?

THESEUS: A moment, my friend. That's a bad beginning, asking in this land of all lands for a king. This city is free. It is not ruled by one man, but by all the people. Each year different people take political office, and the rich have no advantage, for even the poorest have equal rights.

HERALD: More fool you. My city is ruled by one man, not by a rabble. So we don't have people trying to flatter the Assembly and persuading them to do something which only profits the speaker. No; we don't have to put up with the kind of mob orator who is popular one day and perhaps gives good advice, but who ruins the city on the next day with a disastrous proposal, and who then starts accusing other people and laying the blame on them to escape his guilt. How could the *demos* be expected to rule sensibly since it consists of all the ignorant masses? One needs time to develop intelligence – good advice requires lengthy consideration. The poor peasant, even if his poor education doesn't hinder him, hasn't got the time to attend properly to the business of government.

THESEUS: Fine words. But, take it from me, a tyrant or king is the worst evil that can befall a city. Under a tyrant the law is not the law of the people but the decision of one man and so there is no equality. Now if the laws are written, instead of being simply the commands of a tyrant, then both rich and poor are protected by them.

[Euripides, *Suppliants* 399 ff.]

The pride of the Athenians in their city of freedom is worth stressing, not least since such patriotism is rather out of fashion today.

Pericles' funeral speech

The most famous speech concerning Athenian democracy is one that the historian Thucydides records that Pericles made, when he was *strategos*, at a funeral ceremony for those killed in the first year of a war against Sparta. Part of it goes as follows:

> Our government is an original one, modelled on none of our neighbours; indeed others have copied us, but we have copied nobody. We are called a democracy because the whole people and not a minority rule; in the law courts everyone is equal before the law. We appoint our public officials with reference to their merit or ability and not to their family background. No one, not even if he is poverty-stricken, is kept out of politics if he has something to contribute...we have a great many opportunities in our state for simply relaxing, since we have religious festivals and public holidays throughout the year; our private homes are decent and tasteful ...the greatness of our city means that we get everything imaginable imported, so we take foreign luxuries just as much for granted as anything that we can produce at home.

22. *Pericles*

When it comes to military training we can teach our enemies a thing or two as well: our city is open to everybody, and we do not put restrictions on foreigners, out of fear that some spy might get hold of information that would benefit our enemies. This is because it is courage, not surprise, that is our secret weapon.

And look at the way we bring our children up: the Spartans discipline their children from their earliest years, to make them tough – well, we don't; but we're none the less ready to face a crisis. Just consider: the Spartans have to attack us with a whole lot of allies, whereas we, fighting alone, usually defeat our enemies even when we are campaigning in their territory...we don't waste the present practising to face possible trouble in the future, and yet when it comes to the crunch we're every bit as brave as our enemies.

We love what is noble, certainly, but without extravagance; we cultivate the mind, yes, but we're not physically weak. We don't spend our time boasting about what a rich city this is; we make sure that good use is made of that money. And we don't despise a man just because he's poor, but we do expect him to make some efforts to improve his position. And we expect a man to take part in political life; anybody who does not has no place here. Athenians are interested both in their private lives and in the life of the city as a whole. We, the Athenian people, make the political decisions and matters are always fully debated.

All in all, I have no hesitation in saying that Athens is a shining example to the rest of the Greek world. Our citizens, with ease and versatility, could each of them successfully cope with almost anything. For evidence just look at the power and might of Athens... future generations will be as much amazed by our achievements as people are today.... Remember, then, that happiness depends on freedom and that only courage can preserve any freedom in this war.

[Thucydides, 2.36 ff.]

This is, of course, a political speech, delivered in time of war and designed to boost morale; none the less, we may ask just how much truth it contains. If Athens was so obviously wonderful and glorious, why were so many states at war with her? Were they just envious of her success? And why, if she was so courageous and powerful, did she eventually lose this war?

Problems in Pericles' speech

The points that Pericles makes are not all of the same type. Whether Athens was or was not 'a shining example to the rest of Greece' is a question not of fact, but of opinion, and is something that each of us must decide for himself.

Other points, such as the contrast between the Spartan and Athenian attitude to the upbringing of children, are questions of fact, and in this case Pericles would seem to say no more than the truth. There was no state education at Athens, and indeed no higher education of any kind, if we ignore the lectures of travelling sophists which only the rich could afford to attend. By contrast Spartan children were organised into 'packs' or groups at an early age and rigorously trained in the Spartan tradition of physical toughness. They were even expected to find food for themselves, by stealing if necessary; if caught they were beaten, but not because they had been stealing, as Xenophon, an Athenian admirer of Sparta, makes clear:

> Why, you may ask, if the Spartans believe that stealing is an acceptable thing, do they see that the boy who is caught is whipped with a good many stripes? I reply: Because the boy has failed to steal successfully, and it is a universal practice to punish the learner when he fails to do well what he has been taught to do.
>
> [Xenophon, *The Lacedaimonians* 2.8]

It is also a fact that the Athenians had many public holidays on which festivals to the Gods would take place, and that Athens was able, thanks to her empire, to import many foreign luxuries. Whether her private homes were 'decent and tasteful' is open to doubt but the contrast that Pericles intends is once again with Sparta, the enemy, where the citizens eschewed both luxury and, to a large extent, private domestic life, emphasising rather a communal military brotherhood.

But what of the purely political points? Were the Athenians really all equal and free? Did they really all play a prominent part in politics? These questions become particularly interesting when one realises that the same Thucydides who records the above speech has this to say about Pericles himself:

> Pericles restrained the multitude while respecting their liberty; he led them rather than was led by them...and so, although it was said that the people ruled and Athens was called a 'democracy', in fact the power was in the hands of the most prominent citizen, Pericles.
>
> [Thucydides, 2.65 ff.]

The comic poet Aristophanes also takes a dig at Pericles, as if he alone were responsible for the great war that broke out between Athens and Sparta. In the following scene from the *Acharnians* that same Dicaiopolis whom we have already met at the Assembly blames Pericles for the war, as though the *Ecclesia* had had nothing to do with the decision:

DICAIOPOLIS (addressing the audience): Gentlemen, forgive me for talking to you about our city Athens in the middle of a comedy, but even a farce can have a grain or two of truth in it.... Now don't get me wrong: I'm no Spartan sympathiser; I hate them. All I'm saying is: why are we only blaming the Spartans for this war? It was some Athenians – now pay attention there, I didn't say the city as a whole, not all the Athenians; I said *some* Athenians – worthless

23. *Nobility without Extravagance: The Temple of Athene Nike*

scum, who had a grievance against our neighbouring city, little Megara.... Then some drunken idiots went and stole a Megarian prostitute, so the Megarians, in a fury, came here and carried off a couple of whores who were under the care of Pericles' mistress, Aspasia. It was because of the kidnapping of these whores that the war started, because then Pericles, God Almighty himself, raged round making laws excluding Megara from all the markets of the Empire. The Megarians began to starve and so they had to ask Sparta to help them – that's how the war began.

[Aristophanes, *Acharnians* 496 ff.]

We see incidentally from this extract, as from many others, that libel laws can hardly have existed in Athens; but our immediate question is: how much is this charge against Pericles simply a joke? How much truth is there in the suggestion that government was really in the hands of the foremost citizen – an orchestration of power by Pericles? Now is the time to examine exactly what democracy meant in practice for the ordinary Athenian, to look for the truth behind the fine words, and then to try and understand the position of Pericles.

The people in Attica

There were about fifty thousand citizens in Attica in the middle of the fifth century. At the age of eighteen a boy, provided that both his parents were Athenian citizens, took an oath similar to the following and thereupon became a citizen with the right to attend the Assembly and to take on other political office when he reached the required age:

> I will not abandon my fellow citizens in battle; I will fight for my Gods and my home, with my fellow-citizens, or alone if needs be. I will leave my country greater and stronger, not weaker, than it was when I became a citizen. I shall obey such commands as the magistrates see fit in their wisdom to give. I shall obey the laws, both those that exist now and any that shall be added by a unanimous vote of the people; and I will fight on behalf of these laws against any who should try to overthrow them or disobey them. I will respect the Gods and religious customs of my fathers.

Metics, foreigners living permanently in Athens, of whom there may have been twenty thousand, were not citizens, although they were expected to fight in time of war and to pay a special tax. Not being citizens meant that they could play no part in the decision-making of the state; they could not attend the Assembly nor become magistrates, nor were they allowed to own property. Presumably it was the sense of freedom and the opportunity to share in the commercial prosperity of Athens which attracted so many foreigners to settle there.

Slaves

Slaves, perhaps as many as one hundred thousand, were naturally not citizens, but they were nonetheless an important feature of the Athenian way of life. We know that one or two citizens owned a great number of slaves – the general Nicias, for instance, apparently possessed one thousand whom he hired out to work in the silver mines – but such men seem to have been the exception rather than the rule. We may assume that on average even the poor farmer, working his own small plot of land, would have one or two slaves to

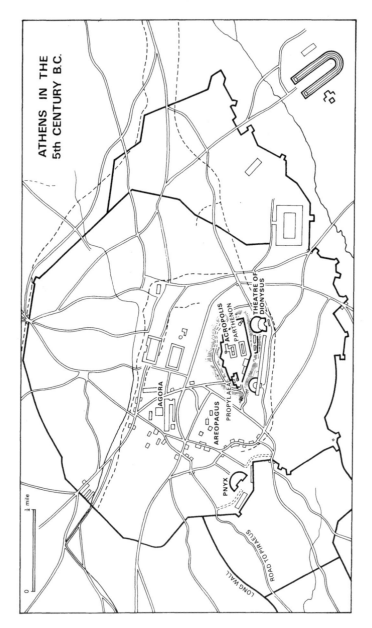

ATHENS IN THE 5th CENTURY B.C.

AGORA

AREOPAGUS

PNYX

ACROPOLIS

PARTHENON

PROPYLAEA

THEATRE OF DIONYSUS

LONG WALL

ROAD TO PIRAEUS

¼ mile

0

24. *Plan of Athens*

help him. Treatment of slaves must have varied from individual to individual, but there is evidence to suggest that the overall picture is a great deal less brutal than, say, that of the eighteenth-century slave trade. The Old Oligarch had this to say on the subject:

> There is a complete lack of discipline amongst the slaves at Athens; you can't get away with hitting them there, and don't expect a slave to make room for you in the *agora:* he won't. I will tell you why this is: if it were standard practice that a citizen should be entitled to strike a slave it would cause chaos, since people would forever be hitting fellow citizens by mistake, thinking that they were slaves. And that's because the people at Athens are no better dressed than the slaves, nor do they look any better off...slaves are important at Athens...and that is why there is freedom of speech between them and their masters. [Old Oligarch 1.10 ff.]

No doubt the Old Oligarch exaggerates to make his point, but the same sort of picture is given by Aristophanes in his comedies.

25. & 26. *Slaves*

One of the most interesting things about the Athenian system of government is that, although slaves were not citizens, some of them were used to act as permanent secretaries to the magistrates; as such they were responsible for keeping records. Most peculiar of all to us, the entire police force consisted of slaves. The band of Scythian bowmen who formed the force could not act on their own initiative: they were dependent on the orders of a magistrate. All the same, to entrust such a job to slaves indicates an attitude to them that we might not normally expect. It also shows us that the Athenian citizen himself regarded police work of a basic kind as unattractive and unsuitable for a free man.

Slaves, then, were clearly important to the Athenian way of life: they did the really unpleasant jobs, such as working in suffocating conditions in the silver mines; they did the unwelcome jobs, such as policing the state; and

27. *The workshop of a bronze sculptor*

most citizens, working as farmers or tradesmen, would benefit from a work-mate who did not require much pay and who could carry on if the master needed to attend something like a meeting of the Assembly. Having slaves to carry on the business was important since there were no large industrial firms in Athens. For the most part a man worked on his own as shoemaker or potter, or whatever it might be, apart from a little slave labour.

However it would be quite wrong to assume that all the real work was done by slaves while the citizens lounged about in the *agora* or on the Pnyx. We have already seen that Pericles was very concerned to create employment for those citizens who did not already have it, by his building programme. That was because they needed to get money from somewhere to live; there was no unemployment benefit. We are lucky to have had preserved the accounts of payment for work done on some of those buildings, and these reveal that citizens, metics and slaves were all working alongside each other at the same rate of pay. Pericles also encouraged the founding of colonies abroad as a way of providing a livelihood for citizens who would otherwise have been unemployed and starving; but to go out as a colonist required considerable determination and hard work once one arrived on some foreign shore. Being a citizen of Athens certainly had its advantages, but it was not an easy life lived entirely at the expense of others.

The position of women

Historians are not agreed about the status of women in all respects. Aristophanes wrote two comedies (the *Lysistrata* and the *Ecclesiazusae*) in which the plot hinges upon women taking over control of the *polis* from men, and it might be assumed that women in Athens therefore behaved in the same sort of way and had the same sort of freedom as men. I, however, would argue

28. *Women working wool*

that Aristophanes' plays only become funny if one assumes that the women in them are represented as behaving in a most unusually free and open manner. It is not certain that they were allowed to attend the theatre in real life. (They certainly did not act. Men played all the parts, but, as masks were always worn, it was easy enough to play female parts.) The pictures of women that we have on vases all seem to show them performing tasks essentially concerned with the home, and one of the girls in the *Lysistrata* talks as if a woman's place was normally expected to be in the home: 'But, my dear, you know how difficult it is for a woman to get out: there's your husband to look after, the slaves to be watched, the children to be fed.'

Lysistrata herself gives the same sort of picture in this passage, in which she also makes it absolutely clear that, whatever else they did, women did not have the right to attend the Assembly:

> LYSISTRATA: Ever since this tedious war started, we women, with a great deal of difficulty and strain, have somehow managed to control ourselves despite everything that you men have done. We never grumbled, never complained; but not because we thought you were

being sensible; no, only because we know how to treat men, and we know they don't like being corrected. Day after day we'd listen to your pompous pronouncements; but, hiding our horror at this war, we'd smile sweetly, and innocently ask whether there was any talk about peace in the Assembly that day. And you would reply with a snarl: 'Don't meddle in men's affairs.'...Obediently I kept quiet. But then you'd make some decision that was even more absurd, and, unable to control myself completely, I'd give a little sigh and say: 'But did you *have* to make a decision like that!' And what was your reply? 'Get on with your spinning. That's a woman's job. War is man's business.'   [Aristophanes, *Lysistrata* 507 ff.]

It is difficult to avoid the conclusion that a woman's life resembled that of women in Victorian England rather than that of women today. In the words of Pericles:

A woman does well if in all respects she lives as the Gods expect and require: that is to say that she should never be the subject of talk amongst men, whether they should be criticising or praising her.
                    [Thucydides 2.45 ff.]

At any rate, one thing we do know: women could not be magistrates, nor could they be members of the *Boule*, nor attend the *Ecclesia* or the courts. They had nationality and certain civil rights, but no active political rights.

So, in talking about the freedom and equality of the Athenians and their political life, we are talking primarily about the adult male citizens. A few of these, such as Nicias and Pericles, were rich men who owned large country estates. The vast majority, however, can be divided into two groups: those who were moderately well off (the *knight* and *zeugite* classes of Solon's classification) and the *thetic* class, whose income was considerably lower. The middle class would tend to be farmers and therefore living outside the city itself, while the *thetes* might find employment either as rowers in the fleet or in one of the many trades going on in the city, as a shoemaker, an armourer, a potter, a carpenter and so on. Despite all that she did achieve, economically speaking Athens remained to the end primitive by modern standards. A village grocery store of today would have amazed an Athenian.

The magistrates

Like any other state, Athens had need of officials to superintend or look after various features of city life. Roads, the markets in the *agora* and the Peiraeus, farming out contracts for the collection of harbour and other taxes, the corn supply imported from abroad without which the Athenians would have starved, the water supply coming from public fountains, and military matters – all these needed close attention. Yet there was never such a thing as a permanent 'Ministry of Taxation' or 'Ministry of Defence'. The people were to retain direct control over everything, and therefore, every year, different people were elected to take responsibility for the various departments. Generally ten magistrates were required for each particular job. Thus every year ten different citizens would be appointed *poletai* (responsible for farming

29. *A fountain house*

out public contracts), another ten would be appointed *logistai* (accountants), others market inspectors, commissioners of weights and measures, corn commissioners and so forth. It was no part of the Athenian system for somebody to make a career of, say, being a market inspector. A man's job might be anything from running a farm to making shoes; a magistracy was something that anybody might expect to take up for a year of his life, during which time he would be paid a small amount to compensate him for what he was not earning; the payment also ensured that even the poorest would be able to play their part.

According to Aristotle there were altogether about seven hundred magistracies within Attica, and the only qualification needed was that a citizen be over the age of thirty. The majority of the magistracies were filled by the drawing of lots between all those who were candidates. There was no question therefore of anybody being expected to have professional qualifications or abilities. According to Xenophon, Socrates thought that this system of electing people to magistracies by lot was foolish: 'Nobody', he said, 'would draw lots to decide who should be captain of a ship, or a carpenter or a musician, although it would matter a great deal less if we did elect our carpenters in this way than it does to elect our magistrates as we do.' [Xenophon, *Memorabilia*, 1.2.9.] Perhaps he had a point, but in fairness it must be admitted that, although anybody might become a magistrate, at the end of their year of office they were subjected to a close examination by the *logistai* to make sure that they had conducted affairs responsibly. The essential point was that, while possibly this was not the most efficient way to organise matters, equality between the citizens was real.

30. *Allotment tokens*

The situation is slightly different with the most important magistracies, namely the generalship (*strategia**) and certain posts concerned with finances. Technically, some of these, the Treasurers of Athena, for example, seem to have still been reserved for members of the wealthiest class, since Solon's law had never been formally withdrawn. In fact, on the one hand, it seems that this law and other similar restrictions on appointments to magistracies began to be ignored during the second half of the fifth century; but, on the other, at least two factors tended to keep these senior magistracies in the control of the prominent and wealthy: first, election to them (e.g. the generalship and the *hellenotamiai*) was dependent on a vote in the Assembly.

---

*Strategia We first hear of the *strategia* (generalship) following Cleisthenes' reforms (see above p. 20). Each of the ten tribes elected one military commander. A problem arises, however, in that for certain years we have evidence that only nine of the tribes had a general, and that one of the nine had two. The earliest date at which we know of this happening is 441 BC, when Pericles' tribe elected two generals, one of whom was Pericles himself. It has been suggested that Pericles was elected by all the people as a supreme commander in view of his pre-eminence, but that view meets with little support today. An alternative explanation is that, since Pericles was being continually re-elected by his tribe, it was felt that from time to time that tribe might elect two generals so as to give others a chance of holding office. It is also possible that by the second half of the fifth century the voting was done by the citizen body as a whole rather than by tribes. Such an arrangement might have resulted in a tendency for one man to be elected from each tribe, without its being the necessary pattern.

Further points worth bearing in mind about the *strategia* are that a *strategos* might take a naval as well as a land command; that when more than one *strategos* was sent on a campaign they had equal authority; and that at the end of his year of office each *strategos*, like other magistrates, was subject to *euthyna* (giving public account of his period in office). Most of the notable political figures of the fifth century served as general for part of their career; most of them came to prominence as generals.

Secondly, since there was no payment for these senior magistracies, they tended to be filled by the wealthier citizens. The Old Oligarch comments:

> The mass of the people steer clear of those magistracies which are of critical importance for the welfare of the whole community and which, if they were mishandled, would lead the city to ruin; they don't, for instance, think that the generals should be appointed by lot. They realise that it is in their interests to leave these posts in the hands of the most influential citizens, but the people as a whole are very keen on holding the salaried magistracies which bring them a certain profit. [Old Oligarch 1.3 ff.]

The fact that all magistrates were either elected by the whole people or appointed by lot every year, that all citizens were in theory eligible for them and a magistracy could not be held twice (once again with the exception of the *strategia*), made the political equality of all a very real thing, and must have tended to make the officials of the state seem very much less remote than they do to most of us today. The citizen, perhaps dealing with a market inspector, might reflect that the following year he himself could well be that magistrate. It is therefore perhaps rather surprising to discover that Aristophanes often makes fun of magistrates, and particularly of the Scythian police accompanying them. The following scene from the *Lysistrata*, while it involves a *proboulos*, which was a special and unusual appointment rather than a regular magistracy, nonetheless illustrates this tendency. The *proboulos* enters to find that the women, who are going on a sex strike to try and force their husbands to stop the war, have barricaded themselves in on the Acropolis, which was where the state funds were kept.

> MAGISTRATE: What a pass things have come to; here I am, a magistrate, come to get some money out of the state treasury to pay for some naval equipment and these women slam the door in my face. Action. Bring me a crowbar. Right now, all together, one, two, three.
>
> LYSISTRATA: There's no need to use force; I'm coming freely. And why use crowbars? You don't need them. What you want is common sense.
>
> MAGISTRATE: Is it just. Scythians, where are you? Right, arrest this woman. Tie her hands behind her back.
>
> LYSISTRATA: If that public servant so much as puts the tip of a finger near me I'll make him a public laughing stock.
>
> MAGISTRATE: Come on, you Scythian, are you frightened of her? Give him a hand, you; grab her round the middle.

31. *Sophocles, who is known to have been elected* strategos *once*

(Enter Calonice)

CALONICE: Lay one hand on her and I'll stamp your guts out.

MAGISTRATE: Charming. Here, one of you, get hold of this one as well.

(Enter Myrrhine)

MYRRHINE: If it's a nice juicy steak for a black eye you'll be wanting, just lay a finger on her.

MAGISTRATE: *Another* one? Where are those Scythians? Get her too. I'll put a stop to all this.

(Enter Stratyllis)

STRATYLLIS: One step towards her and I'll pull the pubics out of that public slave.

MAGISTRATE: Oh my God, I haven't got enough archers for this job. But I'm not going to be defeated by women. Scythians, close your ranks and get them.

LYSISTRATA: I warn you that there are four whole brigades of women behind me.

MAGISTRATE: Right, Scythians, at 'em; tie 'em up.

LYSISTRATA: All right, my comrades in arms, every one of you, bread sellers, barmaids, garlickycabbagyeggysellers, bash them, hit, kick, strike and scratch the enemy. Good, that's it. Now retreat; we mustn't mutilate the dead.

MAGISTRATE: Hmmm. That was a very fine force of Scythians... once. [Aristophanes, *Lysistrata* 421 ff.]

So much for the magistrate, who might very well have been Aristophanes himself one year, just as the dramatist Sophocles is known to have been elected *strategos* once. But the real political power did not lie with the magistrates, who always had to remember that at the end of their year of office they would have to give account of their activities to their fellow citizens. The ultimate power of the state lay with all the citizens in the Assembly, while in practice the Council (*Boule*) was also crucially important, a fact which the Athenians themselves seemed to have recognised when they began the practice of opening their official decrees with the words: 'It has pleased the Assembly and the Council of the Athenian people....'

The *Boule*

The five hundred councillors, elected each year from candidates over the age of thirty, fifty by each tribe, were responsible for keeping a check on the magistrates and for organising the meetings of the Assembly, as well as acting as the figurehead of the state when such things as foreign embassies had to be met. Once again, every citizen was eligible and nobody could be elected more than twice in his life, so in theory every man could expect to have his turn at the hub of events. An example of the *Boule* in action is provided by an interesting story about Pericles' ward (and relative), the brilliant but wayward Alcibiades. In opposition to Nicias, who was then one of the *strategoi*, Alcibiades was anxious that Athens should have an open rift with Sparta; Plutarch continues the story:

At that moment an embassy arrived from Sparta, which was a lucky coincidence for Nicias. They came with some reasonable proposals as a basis for negotiations and they had full powers to make arrangements there and then; they first had a meeting with the *Boule*, where their proposals were warmly received, and a meeting of the Assembly was arranged for the next day, at which the Spartan embassy would be able to put its proposals to the people as a whole.

32. *Aristophanes: comic playwright and author of many of the extracts in this book*

But Alcibiades, afraid that the Athenian people and the Spartan embassy might see eye to eye on the matter, managed to meet the ambassadors privately. He told them that they were being foolish. 'Surely you know,' he said, 'that our Council always receives people first with great politeness and reasonableness, but the full

44

Assembly of the people is a great deal less polite and considerably more demanding; so, if you get up in the Assembly and tell them straight-away that you have unlimited power to come to terms with us, the people will immediately think that they can pressurise you into making enormous concessions. So I suggest that you tell them

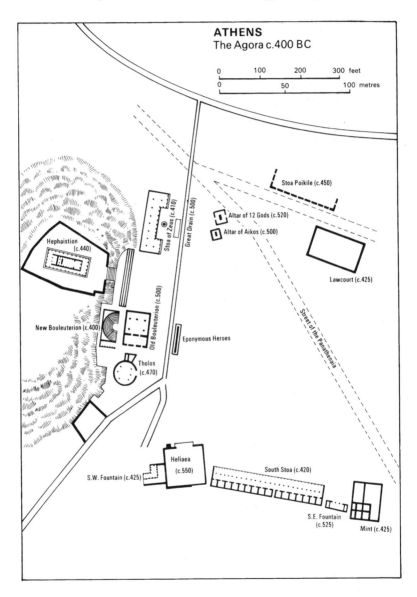

ATHENS
The Agora c.400 BC

0   100   200   300 feet
0   50   100 metres

Stoa Poikile (c.450)

Stoa of Zeus (c.410)

Great Drain (c.500)

Altar of 12 Gods (c.520)

Altar of Aikos (c.500)

Hephaistion (c.440)

Lawcourt (c.425)

Old Bouleuterion (c.500)

New Bouleuterion (c.400)

Eponymous Heroes

Street of the Panathenaia

Tholos (c.470)

Heliaea (c.550)

South Stoa (c.420)

S.W. Fountain (c.425)

S.E. Fountain (c.525)

Mint (c.425)

33. *Plan of the* Agora

tomorrow that, though you are able to discuss things in principle, any specific agreements will have to be referred back to Sparta.'

The next day the Assembly met and the *prytaneis* presented the embassy to the people. The ambassadors, who had fallen for Alcibiades' trick and who trusted him completely, when asked what powers they had, replied that they had not come with full powers to arrange a settlement. Whereupon Alcibiades denounced them as liars and traitors, who couldn't be relied on to say the same thing from one day to the next. The Council, who the day before had heard the ambassadors say the opposite, were outraged; the people were furious, and Nicias, who had supported them, was amazed and generally discredited.   [Plutarch, *Nicias* 10 and *Alcibiades* 14.]

Normally, of course, the *Boule* would not have to experience such dramatic scenes. Demosthenes, a fourth-century orator, describing another real event, gives a straightforward account of how the Athenian people would deal with a political matter that arose urgently, the sort of thing that today would probably be dealt with by a Cabinet of Ministers.

A messenger came to the *prytaneis* and told them about the capture of Elateia. The next day the *prytaneis* summoned the rest of the *Boule*, while the citizens assembled on the Pnyx. Actually the whole *demos* was already waiting there before the *Boule* had worked out an agenda. The Council then left the *Bouleuterion*, walked across the *agora* and up to the Pnyx and finally the herald asked who wanted to address the Assembly. In fact on this occasion nobody spoke, although all the *strategoi* and all the usual speakers were there.   [Demosthenes, *On the Crown*, 169 ff.]

The *Ecclesia*

The passage from Demosthenes shows beyond all doubt that it really was the case that all citizens were directly involved in the government of Athens, but the last sentence, referring to 'the *strategoi* and all the usual speakers', indicates that in practice certain prominent people, such as the *strategoi* (who had after all been elected by the people) and others who made a habit of speaking, would be more likely to have something to say than any Tom, Dicaiopolis or Harry. But they did not have any more right to speak than anyone else. Everybody had the right, and, because Athens was small by any modern standards, they also had the opportunity.

There was no payment for attending the Assembly (although there was during the next century), so it is certainly possible that some, particularly those who had some way to come, did not always attend; however, we do not have to assume that at an average meeting the place would be filled only with town-dwellers. The regular meetings, four in each *prytany*, started early in the morning; people who wanted a good place near the front would therefore have to get up early. Apart from the councillors and the generals who would take up their position at the front, there was no organisation at the *Ecclesia*. A man would stand, perhaps with his friends, wherever he happened to find himself, although Plutarch tells us that one of the aristocratic leaders, Thucydides,

34. *A close-up of the rostrum on the Pnyx*

did attempt to organise his supporters: 'He tried to stop the aristocratic supporters finding themselves haphazardly dotted about the assembly, as they had done in the past, because that had meant that their influence did not make itself felt amongst the large number of the *demos*. He collected them together in one group so that they could make themselves heard and so that they would be noticed.' But in general the Athenian assembly would resemble more the haphazard gathering at a union meeting today than anything that we might associate with our government or Houses of Parliament.

One of Aristophanes' plays is very much concerned with the *Ecclesia*: it is called the *Ecclesiazusae* ('The Females in Assembly'). The heroine, Praxagora, disgusted with the way things are going and convinced that the city's troubles are basically due to the fact that men do all the ruling, has decided that women should take over the *polis*. As the plot unfolds the modern reader is incidentally introduced to many details about the way the Assembly was conducted, including even a reference to the sacrifice to the Gods which always preceded business and the sacred wreath which anyone who wished to speak had first to put on his head.

It is in the dark of the early morning and the women are assembling together in a street near the *agora*:

PRAXAGORA: Silence, everybody. We have got to decide on our plan of action while it's still dark, because this Assembly is due to start at dawn.

1ST WOMAN: Yes, by Zeus, and we must get to the front, right in front of the rostrum where the *prytaneis* will sit.

2ND WOMAN: Now look how sensible I've been: I've brought some wool to card while the Pnyx is filling up.

PRAXAGORA: While people are assembling there? Are you mad?

2ND WOMAN: What's wrong? By Artemis, I can card wool and listen at the same time, can't I? I'm not stupid; besides what about my poor little children who've hardly got anything to wear?

PRAXAGORA: But don't you see – you'd be giving the whole game away if you sit there carding wool; we mustn't give away one glimpse of our femininity. Just suppose that the Assembly is full and one of us women gets her cloak pulled aside while she's struggling to the front so that someone gets an eyeful. A fine mess we'd be in. Oh, no. We've got to get there first, at the front, all hidden in our husbands' cloaks so that nobody suspects that we're women. We'll put on beards and pretend we're men, just like some of those gays do.

1ST WOMAN: But look, we *are* women, and how are we going to hide that fact when we actually speak in the Assembly?

PRAXAGORA: Easy. They say that the randier you are, the better speaker you are. That makes us pretty good speakers.

1ST WOMAN: I'm not sure. They say that experience counts for a lot....

PRAXAGORA: Exactly; that's why we've met here to practice. Right, put on your beards and we'll start. We haven't got a pig to sacrifice, so, you, be the priest will you and take round that kitten instead. Good. Stop talking over there. Excellent. Very well, now who wishes to address the Assembly?

1ST WOMAN: I do.

PRAXAGORA: Then take the sacred wreath, and good luck. Come on. Why don't you get on with it and say something?

1ST WOMAN: But surely I get a drink first, don't I? I thought that this wreath was the sort of thing worn at drinking parties.

PRAXAGORA: Oh for heaven's sake. I hope you're not going to be so stupid when we are in the real Assembly.

1ST WOMAN: Don't they drink at the Assembly then?

PRAXAGORA: Do you think of nothing else?

1ST WOMAN: I was sure that they did; just look at the laws they pass and it's obvious that they must be blind drunk when they vote on them. They make offerings of wine to the Gods, so I bet they knock a few back themselves; and how could they stick all those prayers at the beginning without a drink or two? Anyway they kick up such a din there that anyone would think they were just a bunch of drunks, and then the Scythian bowmen are always having to throw someone out for disorderly conduct, and it wouldn't surprise me if it was drunk and disorderly conduct.

PRAXAGORA: Go and sit down. You won't do at all; you're far too silly.

(After this scene the rehearsal becomes more effective and finally the women are ready to leave and take their places on the Pnyx)

1ST WOMAN: One more point: They raise their hands in the Assembly when they want to take a vote; now we're not very practised in raising our hands; we're more used to having hands raised against us.

PRAXAGORA: A good point. But just let everybody remember the correct procedure: one arm raised straight up like this. Now pick up your tunics so that they don't drag in the dirt and put on your rough walking shoes, like those tough Spartans wear, and like your husbands wear whenever they go to the Assembly, and we're off. Sing some old folk song as you go along as if you were a group of old farmers coming in from the countryside.

[Aristophanes, *Ecclesiazusae* 84 ff.]

And so the women, led by Praxagora, depart to take over the Assembly (interestingly, their proposals for setting the *polis* to rights amount to a rearrangement on Communist lines).

The law-courts

As well as having direct control over all political decisions in the Assembly, and being able to take their turn as magistrates and members of the *Boule* (including being *expected* to do so, according to Pericles' speech), the citizens also held the ultimate power in their hands. Anybody thought to have committed a crime, whether stealing or high treason, would find himself on trial before his fellow-citizens, in certain cases before the full Assembly or the *Boule*, but generally before the jury-courts. As in the case of the *Boule*, any citizen over the age of thirty could be a juryman (*heliast*) and every year each tribe had to produce six hundred jurymen from its number by lot. This made six thousand in all, and they were divided into separate groups to judge different kinds of case in various parts of the city.

35. *Seats of honour for magistrates and priests in the theatre*

A jury for a particular case would sometimes number as many as fifteen hundred but would usually be about five hundred. This must have been inconvenient in many ways, but at least it cut down the chances of bribery and was certainly relatively representative. There was no judge, though a magistrate would act as chairman; nor were there any barristers or solicitors, although there were professional speech-writers, such as Demosthenes and the *metic* Lysias, who would prepare defence speeches for clients. Nor was it any part of the police force's task, those Scythian slaves, to hunt out the criminal: that was the task of individual citizens, who were expected to make it their business to see that any criminal fellow-citizen was brought to justice.

In many ways it may seem a curious system to us, but once again it ensured that the people really were in control of things. Was the great Pericles unpopular at one stage of his career and thought to have behaved a little dishonestly? Very well, then let the people bring him to trial – and they did. Another very famous trial was that of the philosopher Socrates, at the end of the century, on the charge of leading young men astray and disbelieving in the Gods of the city. We have an account of his defence written by Plato, part of which goes as follows:

> Fellow-citizens of Athens, I ask you one favour: I request that you should forgive me and not shout me down if I defend myself by speaking in the way I generally do, and if I use the sort of words and arguments that many of you have frequently heard me use in the *agora* and elsewhere in the city. But I am over seventy and have never yet appeared before a jury; I'm afraid that I really have no idea what sort of thing I ought to say. So I ask you to listen to me as if I were literally a foreigner who had to speak a language with which you were not familiar. Consider not the style of my phrasing, but only the truth of my words. [Plato, *Apology* 17c ff.]

Towards the end of his speech he adds:

> Well, Athenians, that is the only sort of defence I have to offer. But I should add that I hope nobody will hold it against me, because he remembers how he himself, perhaps, was once before a jury and spent a lot of time crying to the judges and produced his children to win sympathy for himself, not to mention a lot of friends and relations to vouch for him, and that I have not adopted any of these methods to win you over. I hope, I say, that nobody thinking along these lines will be angry with me for not doing the conventional thing, and so vote against me. My friends, I am a man, a human being of flesh and blood like the rest of you. Yes; and I have a wife and children...but I will not bring them here to plead on my behalf... instead I rest my defence on the truth of my words.
>
> [Plato, *Apology* 34c ff.]

The Athenians, in fact, acquired quite a reputation for being rather too keen to spend their days bringing lawsuits against each other and sitting on the juries in order to earn the daily wage of three obols. [Old Oligarch 3.2; Thucydides 1.77.1] In his play the *Wasps*, so called because the citizens swarming about in jury groups and stinging people by a fine remind one of a swarm of wasps, Aristophanes makes fun of this passion of his fellow-citizens. Philocleon is an old man with a certain disease:

> He's got the jury-service fever, worse than anyone ever had it. All the time he needs to be on a jury; it quite breaks his heart if he can't be right in the front row of the jurors. He can hardly sleep at night, and if he does he dreams of the water-clock timing the speeches, his thumb pressing against his fingers as if he were holding the voting pebble to place in one of the two urns, the one marked guilty or the one marked not guilty. [*Wasps* 87 ff.]

Philocleon's son Bdelycleon reckons that his father has got to be cured of this passion, especially since in his opinion the jurymen are really slaves to the political leaders and vote just as they are told to do. But Philocleon denies this. According to him the juries exercise the real power at Athens, as he sets out to prove:

36. *A water-clock: a speech was limited to the time it took for the water to pass from one cup to the other*

Nobody in Athens is as influential as those of us who serve on the juries; who is more fortunate or more feared than us, although for the most part we're the old men of the city? We get up early, but nonetheless there's already some great brute hanging about the place where the jury is going to sit; he sidles up greasily to us with the odd spot of cash, nicked from the state funds, in his hand as a sort of present for us. He pleads and whines for a bit, 'Give us a chance, sir; you understand, I'm sure; it's hard for a fellow; all those temptations.' Such respect he shows us, and he doesn't know us from Heracles (unless he's been tried before). I let him soften me up a bit with the odd coin or two, then I take my place for the trial, but, of course, I don't bother about any promise I may have made to the fellow. I understand all the tricks that the accused will try: the 'have pity on me' bit, the 'but I'm as innocent as snow' line, the fellow who bluffs his way through with a joke, the man dragging his wretched children in to arouse our pity. The snivelling little brutes imploring us to forgive their daddy...now isn't all this true power? [*Wasps* 550 ff.]

If one considers how the magistracies, the *Boule*, the *Ecclesia*, and the law-courts worked in practice, it is difficult not to feel that the *demos* at Athens did indeed have true power.

Payment

All this talk of equality and freedom for every citizen would have been of little use without a system of payment; and for all the talk of the wealth and power of Athens, which was true enough thanks to her Empire, there will

37. *A young man such as Strepsiades' son*

have been many thousands of citizens who had to work pretty hard, on their farms or in their shops, to make ends meet. Take, for instance, the character Strepsiades in Aristophanes' play the *Clouds*. At the opening of the play he is tossing and turning on his bunk-style bed between worn and thin blankets, unable to sleep because of his money problems (largely caused by the extravagance of his playboy son, Pheidippides):

> STREPSIADES: My, God, My God, these miserable nights – they never end. Where's that cock got to, why doesn't he crow or something. Oh I can't sleep, simply cannot. It's these debts: they're biting me through and through, all run up by that splendid boy of mine, snoring and farting away there. He loves horses and so I'm bankrupt...it was marrying his mother that did me. I was doing fine, a cheerful farmer I was, dirty, yes, shabbily dressed, but I was carefree enough with my olives and my sheep, then I had to marry that classy woman. The farmer and high-faluting lady from up town – a lady indeed. I ask you, what a combination: Me stinking of dung and the farm, her of exotic perfumes (and expensive too). Grand

53

ideas she had. You name it, she wanted it, and more of it: perfume, parties, pearls, oh, and of course sex. Wearing me out she was. Then this lad was born...and she had grand ideas for him too. 'When you're a big boy,' she used to whisper, 'you'll drive about in a beautiful carriage.'...That's just fine; the trouble is, he's driving me to ruin.

[Aristophanes, *Clouds* 1 ff.]

How did the Athenians enable a poor man like Strepsiades to take part in political life? and how did they pay for things such as their navy, their roads and their theatre productions?

Attendance at the Assembly was not paid, and no doubt many citizens could not afford to give up the forty or so days a year that regular attendance would require. But it seems likely that individuals would take the trouble to participate when the agenda seemed to them of particular importance. As we have seen, most magistrates and councillors were paid so that all could afford to play their part. Jurymen also were paid the sum of two obols a day, later raised to three. Three obols was not a large sum of money – the workers on the buildings of the Acropolis for instance were paid nearly twice this amount – but some unskilled labourers are known to have been paid as little as three obols a day, so it must have been a living wage, even if a poor one. Altogether, Aristotle reckoned, the state 'paid twenty thousand men every year from the money received as tribute from the allies and from various taxes; there were about six thousand jurymen, the *Boule*, five hundred guards for the dockyards and about seven hundred minor magistrates as well as the orphans of the state who were looked after at the public expense'. Many of those citizens who were not in any official position during a given year would neither pay nor be paid any money. A farmer, for example, might hardly deal with money at all; he simply grew the food his family needed, built the house he lived in, while his wife made the clothes they wore; anything he couldn't produce himself, such as shoes, he might well obtain by bartering other goods. (This is not to say that money was never used, particularly in the urban centre; but barter and exchange were certainly an aspect of rural life.)

However there were rich men, as we have seen, such as Pericles, Nicias and Cimon, who actually gave hand-outs to the people; and, as we shall see, there were expensive things that needed to be done. Instead of having a permanent tax on the rich the Athenians developed a fascinating system of giving specific responsibilities to individuals. Rich citizens were nominated in turn each year to bear the expense for such things as equipping a trireme for the navy, for the training of a chorus to take part in one of the plays at the dramatic festivals and the provision of a feast for the tribe they belonged to at such festivals. This system of *liturgies* (as the responsibilities were called) was of course a considerable strain on the rich, as well as a great advantage to the poor, but it did mean that the rich could point very clearly and with pride to their contribution to the welfare of the community. It was also permissible for an individual to appeal against the *liturgy* if he could show that someone else was better able to bear the cost (a sort of means test in reverse). The person challenged could either accept the duty of performing the *liturgy* or, if he thought that he was not the richer of the two, he could offer to exchange his property with the other man.

38. *An olive harvest*

A speech written by the orator Lysias for a client indicates both how extensive such costs could be for a rich man and also how he might point to his services with pride:

> In 411, when I was appointed to pay for the training of a chorus, I spent 30 minae and then two months later another 2,000 drachmai on a men's chorus. In the next year I spent 800 drachmai on dancers for the great Panathenaic festival and 5,000 on another men's chorus in the same year...meanwhile for seven years running I maintained a trireme and that cost me six talents.   [Lysias 21 ff.]

The speaker goes on to list yet more *liturgies*, and the figures he says that he spent are considerable: he must have been a very rich man.

Isonomia, equal political rights or, as we might say, equality before the law, was something that the Athenians were particularly proud of; it and freedom of speech were two of the things that they regarded as inseparable from democracy. And their political arrangements were clearly designed to make the equality and the freedom real. Rich and poor there certainly were, but the rich had to give more and the poor were not deprived of their rights. It has taken most of the world something like two thousand years to arrive at an arrangement similar to that which the Athenians created in about twenty-five.

39. *A model of a fifth-century country house*

Pericles

What then was this fellow Pericles up to? If Athens was democratic and the people, old Strepsiades and so on, ruled, why do historians talk of 'Periclean Athens' as if he were king of it? And why does Thucydides suggest that during these years Athens was only a democracy in name and not in fact?

There were no political parties in Athens as we should understand the term. That is to say there were no organised parties with an official leader, although naturally there will have been groups of people who were inclined to share the same views. At one point in Aristophanes' *Ecclesiazusae*, Praxagora is applauded by the town mob, while the countryfolk boo her; and no doubt in real life the Assembly sometimes divided itself in this way (particularly perhaps during the war when it was the farmers from the country who suffered most). Often the aristocratic oligarchs must have felt differently from working people about a point of policy. At other times those directly concerned with rowing in the fleet may have had a special point of view, and so on. We have already seen that the politician (not the historian) Thucydides had a band of people who supported him and whom he grouped together in the

Assembly so that they should appear more impressive. Yet Thucydides had no political position. His authority was dependent on his being elected by the people to the *strategia* each year. As one of the ten *strategoi* in any year he had a certain responsibility given him by the people; but each year they could also take it away from him. And even as *strategos*, he still had to get a majority vote from the Assembly for any single act or measure that he wanted to introduce; his party, by which we can only mean his close circle of friends and supporters, counted for no more than the number of hands they could raise in the *Ecclesia*.

Pericles is described as a 'leader of the people' by the Greek historians, not in the sense that we would describe Tony Blair as leader of the Labour party or Prime Minister of Britain, but in the sense that by and large his policies were those that suited the majority of the citizens in the Assembly.

Between 445 BC and his death in 429 BC Pericles was re-elected almost every year by his tribe as *strategos*, and that fact really supplies the answers to the questions about his position; for it will be remembered that the *strategia* was one of the few political offices that was gained by election rather than by the drawing of lots. If Pericles was almost consistently voted for during his life – and he was – then Pericles must have been much respected and very popular. There are obviously several ways in which a statesman can gain popularity: he can give good advice and the people can learn to trust him; he can make extravagant promises of what he will do if he is elected (but if his promises don't come true he is not likely to be re-elected), or he can make himself popular by putting forward proposals which may be irresponsible but which look attractive. In Pericles' case it looks, despite the attacks on him by his enemies, as if the majority of people looked to him in the Assembly for good advice and continued to feel that he was giving it. The result was that although he had no special power, since he was only one of ten *strategoi*, all of whom were subordinate to the *demos* and the laws, he came over the years to enjoy great respect and to be able to be fairly sure of persuading the people to do what he thought best.

To ask whether Athens was really democratic, whether the people really ruled, as some historians have done, is therefore not a very real question. There is indeed one enormously important qualification that must always be borne in mind: the franchise in Athens (and, as far as we know in other democratic Greek cities) was severely circumscribed; women, slaves, and *metics*, which is to say the vast majority of the population, did not have political power. It was confined to free adult male citizens. But in terms of political theory, and indeed practical organisation, the Athenian system indubitably counts as a radical participatory democracy, inasmuch as all citizens effectively shared power and authority equally. The people retained the right to choose freely each year who should be their *strategoi* and to decide on every matter in the Assembly. The fact that Pericles was basically dependent on the goodwill of the people is brought home to us when Thucydides, the historian, tells us that during the first year of the Peloponnesian War there was a great deal of ill-feeling against Pericles:

> And the *demos* were not satisfied until they had condemned him to pay a fine. A little later, however, changing their mind as a crowd is inclined to do, they re-elected him to the *strategia* and allowed him to give the lead in all matters.   [Thucydides 2.65 ff.]

40. *Chorus of knights*

Aristophanes, in his comedy the *Knights*, puts the matter in a nutshell. The people, the citizen body as a whole, are introduced onto the stage in the character of a single man named Demos, and two prominent *strategoi* of the time, Nicias and Demosthenes, are also portrayed; but the significant point is that they are portrayed as *slaves* of the Demos. This is how Demosthenes explains the situation to his audience:

> DEMOSTHENES: Our master is Demos. He's basically a countryman, fond of his greens, and with a passion for the law courts; irritable and difficult to please, quite old and rather deaf. Where does he live? Why, on the Pnyx of course.
>
> [Aristophanes, *Knights* 40 ff.]

While the *Knights*, which was produced in 424 BC clearly maintains a view of the *demos* as the master, it also unmistakeably advances two critical warnings relating to the conduct of the democracy. First, the character Paphlagon, who represents Cleon (also a target in the *Wasps* of 422), is shown as unscrupulously manipulating Demos. Secondly, the chorus of knights explicitly draws attention to the danger of the people, in their arrogance and complacency, being misled:

> Oh, Demos, glorious is your power, when all men fear your authority. Yet you are almost powerless to resist empty flattery and deceit. You are swayed equally by every speaker in turn. Your mind, though none doubt you have one, seems to have taken a vacation.
> [Aristophanes, *Knights* 1111 ff.]

No doubt it would be wise at this point to repeat the observation that Aristophanes, being a comic writer, cannot be used uncritically as direct evidence for the reality of scenes and characters he depicts. Nor, even if he were an historian, should we forget that he had his point of view, such as an obvious contempt for Cleon. Nevertheless, we can hardly ignore either the fact that he held this view or that, apparently, he could please his fellow Athenians by playing on it. Some historians try to dismiss the significance of the widespread, not to say uniform, criticism of Athenian democracy towards the end of the fifth century in our sources, on the grounds that the sources were all anti-democratic. That is too easy and rather begs the question. Some significance should surely be attached to the fact that individuals as diverse as Thucydides and Aristophanes concur in clearly suggesting that, in the last quarter of the century, the *demos* became a prey to a number of self-seeking demagogues.

4
The Peloponnesian War

Demagogues

In 431 BC the League of Peloponnesian states, led by Sparta, fearful and jealous of Athens' new power and strength, went to war with her, and this war effectively lasted until 404 BC. Pericles died in 429 BC. Both these facts had

41. *The enemy:*
a grim-looking Spartan soldier

considerable importance for the nature of the democracy. In the first place, because of the war, the country people had to retire inside the walls surrounding the *polis* itself and joining it with the Peiraeus.

> And since most Athenians, now as well as in the past, were born and bred in the country, they were most upset at having to move lock, stock and barrel into the city.... There was a great reluctance and a feeling of sorrow as they now abandoned their homes and the villages which each regarded as his own city and prepared to meet an entirely new life in Athens itself.   [Thucydides, 2.16 ff.]

Now at any rate there was no reason for the country folk to stay away from the *Ecclesia*.

Yet now, as all our ancient writers bear witness, the quality of the democracy began to decline; and in the opinion of the writer of the Aristotelian *Constitution of Athens* this is largely because of the second point, the death of Pericles:

As long as Pericles was leader of the people the state was well organised; but after his death the situation deteriorated, because up to that time all the leaders of the people were well-to-do and respectable people. But when Pericles died, Cleon became the dominant man in the Assembly, and he more than anybody debased politics by his violent methods; he was the first man to rant and rave and use abuse and insults in the *Ecclesia*. He was followed by Cleophon, and after him there was a whole series of people in popular favour who were notable for their outrageous behaviour and for their desire simply to please the people, caring only about their own popularity and success.

[Aristotle, *Constitution of Athens* 28.1 ff.]

Aristotle was obviously not much impressed by Cleon, judging him from a later date, but Aristophanes, who was living with him in the overcrowded city, soon to be struck by a devastating plague, seems to have loathed him.

42. *A Comic Actor*

He felt that the people were not really in control any more, they were under the thumb of loudmouths like Cleon who, by flattering them, fooling them and putting on a fine display of oratory, completely duped them into doing whatever they, the speakers, wanted. In the *Knights*, as we saw in the last chapter, Demosthenes and Nicias, two real-life generals here depicted as slaves of Demos, are worried about the influence of Paphlagon (Cleon), who is seen to be controlling Demos rather than carrying out his wishes as a servant should.

DEMOSTHENES: Last month our master, Demos, bought a new slave – a fellow called Paphlagon, common as muck and a fantastic con-man and liar as well. It didn't take this Paphlagon long to discover all Demos' weak points; he sucks up to him, flatters, cajoles and persuades; a regular little arse-licker. He's always egging the master on to earn his jury fee by bringing somebody or other up for trial. Only the other day I, Demosthenes, scored a great victory for my master, but would you believe it, this Paphlagon fellow comes rushing in and convinces the master that he should have the credit. He's got the old man right where he wants him; he quotes oracles and prophecies, and Demos believes them; he slanders the rest of us, and Demos believes the lies and turns against us. Then Paphlagon comes to us and says 'See. I'm the one with power over the master; if you want to stay in his good books, I'm the one you want to look after.' So we pay up. If we don't, the master will be sure to punish us on Paphlagon's advice.

[Aristophanes, *Knights*, 43 ff.]

Demosthenes and Nicias realise that the only way to get rid of Paphlagon is to find somebody else even more revolting, who will be able to outdo him in winning the approval of Demos. They find a sausage-seller and set about persuading him that he could easily acquire the influence that Paphlagon has:

DEMOSTHENES: Do you see all those people, the audience, sitting in rows out there?

SAUSAGE-SELLER: Of course.

DEMOSTHENES: You will be the overlord of all those people. In the *agora*, the harbour and on the Pnyx, you will lead them where you want. The *strategoi* will be under your orders, the *Boule* will obey your instructions. The *Prytaneum* will become as good as your private home.

SAUSAGE-SELLER: Me? I shall have all this power?

DEMOSTHENES: You. And more than that. Stand on this a moment, and take a look at all the islands stretching away in the Aegean sea there, all those markets, those ships, and just swivel your eyes from Asia to Africa. See? Now the whole of the great Empire will be in your power, for I have an oracle here that says you will become the Greatest of men.

SAUSAGE-SELLER: You must be joking. I'm just a tradesman; how am I supposed to become one of the high and mighty?

DEMOSTHENES: That's the whole point: you're such a crooked little salesman, so good at heckling in the *agora*, that you're bound to do well in politics.

SAUSAGE-SELLER: No, really, I'm not worthy of this –

DEMOSTHENES: What's that? You're not a respectable sort of chap are you, not well educated or anything like that?

SAUSAGE-SELLER: Oh, no. I come from the worst kind of background.

DEMOSTHENES: Excellent. I can assure you that the worse you are the better your chances of success. It's a slight pity that you know how to spell: that *could* be held against you. The fact is that Demos cannot be led by decent educated people anymore; he only listens to the ignorant and crooked. [*Knights* 163 ff.]

The sausage-seller is finally persuaded that with the help of the *knights*, the middle-class citizens, he will be able to replace Paphlagon in Demos' favour. Then Paphlagon himself enters and furiously denounces the plot against him, as if he were on the Pnyx trying to stir up the people:

PAPHLAGON: Oh, beloved city. Oh, Demos, my Demos, see, see how these wretches are attacking me.

KNIGHTS: There he goes again. The usual mob oratory: shouting and screaming, so that nothing really ever gets done.

SAUSAGE-SELLER: Well, now I shall outshout him.

PAPHLAGON: By God, I lay a charge against this man. I accuse him of being a traitor!

SAUSAGE-SELLER: And I accuse him – of growing fat at the city's expense.

PAPHLAGON: I demand the death penalty for this traitor.

SAUSAGE-SELLER: I can shout three times as loud as you.

PAPHLAGON: I can shout louder than you can shout louder than me. Why, you vile cheat, these are my tricks you're using. I'll accuse you in front of the *prytaneis*. I'll tell them you've got rather a lot stashed away to which you have no right. That'll settle your hash.

KNIGHTS: You cold blooded, loud-mouthed con-man. All Attica, the *Ecclesia*, the Treasury, the law-courts are contaminated by your outrageous behaviour. Athens herself staggers under your ranting and raging. [*Knights* 273 ff.]

Paphlagon and the sausage-seller decided to appeal directly to Demos himself, each confident that the master will reject the other.

DEMOS: What's all this shouting out here? Get away from here, will you? You're breaking the place up. Oh, it's you, Paphlagon; what's up? Is somebody troubling you?

PAPHLAGON: I'm being attacked by the knights and this scum here, and all because of my deep love and concern for you.

DEMOS: And who is this 'scum'?

SAUSAGE-SELLER: I am another of your lovers. For years I have loved you, Demos, and along with many other good men have desperately tried to look after you well, but this Paphlagon prevents us achieving anything. With due respect, master, the trouble is that you are too inclined to take up with the worst sort of people, the lowest kind of tradesmen. Now, Demos....

PAPHLAGON: Call an Assembly and then you'll find out which of us really cares more about you.

SAUSAGE-SELLER: Yes, make a choice between us; but not on the Pnyx.

DEMOS: If I've got to make decisions I'll only do it on the Pnyx. So forward.

SAUSAGE-SELLER: My God, now I'm ruined. When he's at home Demos is a sharp fellow, very reliable and sensible. But once he gets up to the Pnyx he becomes a complete moron, like a child who likes only whoever gives him the most sweets.   [*Knights* 728 ff.]

In fact the sausage-seller finally defeats Paphlagon and the play ends on a less critical note, with Demos made young again and able to judge a little better between his good and bad advisers. Behind the exaggeration and absurdity of the comedy, Aristophanes is clearly suggesting that the democracy was now beginning to resemble something like an unruly mob in the hands of unscrupulous demagogues. Once again (and for the last time) it must be acknowledged that comedy, satire in particular, is not straightforward evidence. Equally, successful comedy and satire that is appreciated by its audience depends upon an exaggeration or distortion of some actual tendency. To depict Cleon as a loud-mouthed braggart, if in fact he was the epitome of modest decorum, could only be funny in some exceptional, and carefully pointed, case. Though no doubt it is overdone, and indeed to Cleon himself and his supporters it might seem without foundation, we surely should presume that if Aristophanes can entertain people with this image of Cleon it is because the majority of people see it as an *appropriate* distortion.

I labour this point because the question of the reliability of our sources becomes rather important in assessing the quality of the democracy at Athens following the death of Pericles. There are those who both want to dismiss comedy (and tragic drama, poetry) as evidence altogether, and to dismiss all other sources as being anti-democratic. They can then draw the conclusion that there is no reason to suppose any decline, or indeed any change, in the workings of the democracy at Athens in the last part of the fifth century.

Why it is so important to them to draw this conclusion, I do not know, though it looks a little bit as if there are people for whom democracy is necessarily good and therefore uncriticisable. But this seems to me bizarre and perverse in the extreme. Comedy is obviously evidence, although it is conceded it must be handled with care. If it is true in this case that all sources are anti-democratic, that in itself surely tells us something. Thirdly, it is far from clear to me that they are all anti-democratic. What they are is uniformly critical of characters such as Cleon and Hyperbolus who came to the fore after Pericles' death. To interpret that as 'anti-democratic' surely begs the question. It seems to me far more plausible to argue that our sources have varying attitudes to democracy as it functioned in Pericles' time, but that they are united in seeing Cleon as a demagogue. Why call that 'bias' rather than 'opinion' or, by extension, 'evidence'? Finally, regardless of difficulties of interpretation, our sources seem to me to present us with a number of fairly straightforward events. And these events, in my view, add up to a picture which suggests that Aristophanes' jokes were not that wide of the mark. Not only was Cleon a new kind of political figure, because of his background and his methods of debating. He also differed from the influential figures of the past in that, to begin with, he seems to have had no official position. When Pericles had spoken in the Assembly he had done so as an elected *strategos*, and although any citizen was entitled to speak, Cleon seems to have been something new in that he set himself up as a regular speaker. He was a member of the Council early in his career, chosen by lot of course, but the people did not actually elect him to be a *strategos* until the very end of his eight or nine years of political activity in the Assembly. His first official command came almost by accident, as Thucydides tells us. The Assembly had met to discuss the situation at Pylos. On a little island there, off the Laconian coast, the Athenians had trapped, but so far failed to capture, a number of Spartan soldiers. The Spartans had offered to make peace in return for the men but Cleon had persuaded the people to reject the offer.

Now the *demos* began to regret that they had rejected the peace terms. And Cleon, realising that he was becoming unpopular for having persuaded the people to do this, now said that the news from Pylos, which reported that the Athenians were finding it difficult to actually capture the Spartans, was false. The messengers therefore suggested that, if the Assembly didn't believe their report, somebody else should be sent out; Cleon was one of the people chosen to go. He now saw that either he would have to bring back the same report or else run the risk of being shown up as a liar. So, seeing that the people were in the mood for action, he said that they shouldn't be wasting time sending out inspectors; they should set sail with more men and capture the Spartans. He then pointed at Nicias, who was one of the *strategoi* for the year and whom he hated, and put all the blame on him, saying that if only the Athenians elected proper *strategoi* they might get something done. Nothing could be easier than to capture a handful of Spartans on an island, he said; he would have done it if he'd been in command.... Nicias replied that, so far as he was concerned, nothing was stopping Cleon taking command of a force and doing so.... Cleon, thinking at first that Nicias couldn't be serious, agreed, but when he realised that Nicias was being serious he began to try and get out of it, saying that Nicias was the *strategos*, not him.... The Assembly, behaving as crowds usually do, became more keen to make Cleon take on the command when they saw that he didn't really want to. Cleon finally had to accept it...and

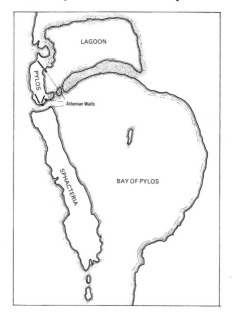

43. *Map of Pylos*

the intelligent members of the Assembly reflected that whatever happened now they would gain something: either Cleon would succeed, which would obviously be good for the city, or, if he failed, that would put paid to him.   [Thucydides, 4.27 ff.]

This passage, of course, besides reaffirming that, while most of the speaking may be done by a few prominent individuals, decisions are made by the people as a whole, is plainly unsympathetic to Cleon. Furthermore, whatever Thucydides' personal view of him, Cleon must have retained popularity with the mass of the people, given that he retained the ear of the Assembly for a number of years. Indeed, Thucydides records that 'at that time (427 BC) he had by far the greatest influence with the *demos*.' [Thucydides 3.36.6]; but while it is evident that Thucydides does not like Cleon, it is also clear both that he can be fair to him (as in recognising his influence), and that he has his reasons for not liking him. We may not share Thucydides' disdain for the way in which this particular command for Cleon came about, but the historian is nonetheless giving us data about how it came about; and we may, perhaps, share the view that this is a rather chancy and peculiar way for a state to be making crucial decisions.

We have no evidence for characters such as Cleon before the war, but we now meet, mainly in the plays of Aristophanes, with a whole list of them. The argument, then, is that Pericles was a reliable leader who managed both

44. *Shield of a Spartan, captured at Pylos*

to give sound advice and to keep the favour of the Assembly, but that, after his death, people like Cleon, Cleophon and Hyperbolus, behaved irresponsibly, often giving bad advice for selfish reasons. We cannot be sure that it is as simple as that: we do not have so much evidence for the early years; most of the writers who criticise the later years were, by birth, and probably inclination, aristocratic; and then the war will obviously have made some difference to the behaviour of the people. However, we cannot get away from the fact that the picture painted by the writers we have is deeply critical. Thucydides tells more or less the same story as Aristotle:

> Pericles' successors were less notable than he and were all concerned
> to advance themselves; they adopted cheap political tactics and so
> failed to control affairs properly; naturally many mistakes were made.
> [Thucydides 2.65 ff.]

An example of the sort of mistake the Athenians began to make, according to Thucydides – though he adds that there were many others, unspecified – was the military invasion of far-off Sicily which took place in 415 BC, and which ended in disaster two years later. The man who really promoted this enterprise was Alcibiades, who, some said, was dreaming of extending the Athenian Empire as far as Carthage. Some may have felt that the very proposal smacked of *hubris*; others that it was hazardous and not of obvious advantage to the Athenians. It is certainly arguable that the expedition was at odds with the strategy that Pericles had advocated. However, although Thucydides reports Nicias' argument against 'undertaking a war that does not concern us' [Thucydides 6.9.1] and remarks that the Athenians made their

45. *A Restoration of the South Peristyle of the Parthenon*

decision largely 'in ignorance of the size of Sicily and the large number of its inhabitants' [Thucydides 6.1], he tends to the view that the blundering lay not with the original decision, so much as with the mismanagement of the operation once the decision had been made. Nicias was one of the *strategoi* and he was utterly opposed to the idea; yet, against his advice and wish, he was sent, because the people did like it. Alcibiades, who did want to go, was recalled as soon as he arrived, on a charge of sacrilege.

The enterprise failed, according to Thucydides, because:

> The speakers in the Assembly at home were more concerned with fighting each other for the favour of the *demos* than anything else; by arguing with each other they let the affairs of the city become ignored.... Indeed, in the end the only reason that the Athenians lost the war against Sparta was because they destroyed themselves by squabbling amongst themselves. [Thucydides 2.65 ff.]

Informers

Another sign that all was not well was the way in which the system of legal prosecution was getting out of hand. Throughout the fifth century the Athenians had had no state prosecution system; it was left to individual citizens to make charges against their neighbours, if there were grounds. There were tremendous penalties attached to anyone who made an accusation which was not upheld in the courts, and this must have deterred people from making false or frivolous charges. Even so, it seems that towards the end of the century people were getting away with making outrageous accusations: to such an extent that, to Aristophanes at least, there appeared to be a number of people who almost made a living out of informing on others; for if an accusation was upheld in the courts the accuser was entitled, as a reward, to a share of the fine imposed on the guilty.

Dicaiopolis has a spot of trouble with an informer. He has made his private peace with the enemy and is therefore trading with a half-starved Megarian, who is trying to sell his daughters dressed up as pigs. The informer enters:

> INFORMER: O.K., who are you? Give an account of yourself.
>
> MEGARIAN: I'm a Megarian pig-seller.
>
> INFORMER: Right, then I'll denounce you and your pigs as enemies of the Athenian people.
>
> MEGARIAN: Oh, God, here we go again: the very source of all our troubles.
>
> INFORMER: You'll pay for being Megarian. Let go of that sack.
>
> MEGARIAN: Help, Dicaiopolis, help. An informer. Help me.
>
> DICAIOPOLIS: Where is he? Why don't the *agora* officials keep these creatures out? What the hell are you up to?
>
> INFORMER: Now look here. It is our duty to expose enemies....
>
> DICAIOPOLIS: Get out, do you hear? Go and expose somebody else. Out. Out.   [Aristophanes, *Acharnians* 818 ff.]

In Aristophanes' *Ploutos*, Chremylos has trouble with an informer; but it is the threats made by the informer that are of interest here. Chremylos has restored sight to the blind God Ploutos (Wealth), with the result that money is now only distributed to good citizens, and people like the informer have been deprived of any chance of making a fortune by their evil trade.

> INFORMER: I'm going, don't worry. But I'll be back. If I can just lay my hands on a witness I'll lay a charge against this God of yours, this Ploutos fellow. By Zeus, it's as clear as crystal that he's going

to overthrow the democracy. He'll ignore the *Boule* and the Assembly, and set himself up as a dictator before we know where we are.

[Aristophanes, *Ploutos* 944 ff.]

Informers should probably not be thought of as we might think of them in the context of a police state. In the absence of any kind of detective agency or investigative police force as we know it, informers were the prime source of detection (or 'policing' in one sense of the word). Furthermore, from the democratic point of view, there was good reason to remain vigilant about possible oligarchic anti-democratic activity. However, despite the fact that informers thus have a quasi-legitimate place in the Athenian political arena, Aristophanes at least (allowing as always for comic exaggeration) would seem to think that too many people were too ready to throw out charges of 'traitor to the people' and 'enemy of democracy' against fellow-citizens.

Some actual decisions of the people

Demagogues, informers, irresponsible decisions in the Assembly, hysterical fears of revolution against the Democracy: that is the highly-coloured picture that we can find in Aristophanes. Comedy always exaggerates, but it generally builds on truth. To assess this view point we must look briefly at some of the things that were going on in the Assembly during the last thirty years of the century.

The most famous example that we have of the Assembly in action during Cleon's supremacy occurred in 427, when the Peloponnesian war had been going on for three years. The city of Mytilene had revolted from the Athenian Empire but had then been reduced by the general Paches, who sent to Athens to enquire from the Assembly what he should do next.

> The Assembly discussed what they should do and in their anger decided to put to death both the hostages whom Paches had sent and also every single adult male in Mytilene, and to enslave all the women and children.... They sent a trireme to Paches to inform him of what had been decided. On the next day, however, the people changed their minds and began to think that their decision had been cruel and unprecedented. Some representatives from Mytilene, noting this change of mood, approached the *Boule* in order to get another Assembly called; they succeeded because the Council saw for themselves that most people wanted another chance to discuss the matter. So an Assembly was called at once and various speakers offered different points of view. Cleon, who had argued the previous day in favour of putting the Mytileneans to death, spoke again. He

was a violent sort of man, but also very influential with the people. He said: 'Several times in the past I've had my doubts about democracy when it comes to controlling an empire, and I'm more doubtful than ever now that I see you changing your minds about Mytilene. The trouble is that because here in Athens we all live alongside each other without fear or intrigue you are too trusting to your allies, and assume that they are equally open and trustworthy.

46. *The owl: the symbol of Athene*

A policy of mercy on this occasion would be weakness, and weakness is dangerous. You seem to forget that your rule over the empire is a dictatorship over subjects who don't like it and who are always watching for an opportunity to escape it. They will obey only so long as you are stronger.'   [Thucydides 3.36 ff.]

On this occasion Cleon failed to carry the Assembly with him. A man called Diodotus opposed him and succeeded in persuading the *Ecclesia* to vote that another trireme should be sent out to overtake the first and cancel the order to put all the male prisoners to death. The point of this episode for us is that, besides illustrating that the Assembly makes the final decision, it also shows how easily it might change its mind, for good or bad, from one day to the next. It also seems to indicate that individual speakers might exert considerable influence; Cleon, for instance, seems to have persuaded them one way on the first day, and Diodotus another way on the second day.

Incidentally, it would be wrong to overstress what must strike us as the cruelty of Cleon's proposals. Certainly some Athenians did feel that to kill all the men was going too far – that was why the second Assembly had been called. But Diodotus (at least according to Thucydides) did not attempt to discredit Cleon by arguing that such measures were savage; he simply claimed that Cleon had miscalculated and that in fact it would pay Athens better in the long run to have been seen to be lenient. The Greeks were a great deal less disturbed by the idea of cruelty than we are: warfare was something that most of them grew up with; the exposing of new-born children on the mountainside was an accepted method of birth control. They did not practice the kind of pointless savagery that the Romans did when they watched gladiators destroying each other or wrestling with wild animals, but they could be savage enough when there seemed reason to be so. At the beginning of the war, for instance, the Spartans killed anybody captured at sea [Thucydides 2.67.4]. And eleven years after the Mytilenean debate, the Athenians were to put to death all the male inhabitants of the island of Melos because originally it wanted to remain neutral. There were no second thoughts this time. [Thucydides 5.84 ff.]

There are other examples which might make some wonder whether government by the whole people was proving either reasonable or reliable. The generals who were in command of the siege of the town of Potidaea made terms with the city without sending back to Athens to await orders from the Assembly. The Athenian people were furious and felt that better terms of surrender could have been acquired than in fact were. They may have been right, of course; but the generals were on the spot more than a hundred miles from home, and the fact that all generals were supposed to await instruction from home even when on campaign must have caused some dangerous delays. We do not know what happened to these generals, but of three others, who made a peace without consulting the Assembly, 'two were banished and one was fined because the Athenians thought that they must have been bribed to leave Sicily, since they could easily have captured the whole island'. Again, we do not know that they had not been bribed, but we can be pretty sure that only Athenians at home who had never been to Sicily, which is a large place, could possibly have believed that the whole island might have been conquered. Was it sensible to get rid of generals every time they failed to do what the people, often in ignorance of the actual situation, wanted? It is not surprising that the general Demosthenes, after an admittedly disastrous campaign, did not dare to return to Athens 'since he was afraid to face the people'. 'Oh, Demos,' as Aristophanes said, 'glorious is your power when all men fear your authority'.

By 411 BC things were going badly for Athens. Her great expedition to Sicily had failed, and as a result many members of her empire, thinking that she was on her knees, revolted. At this juncture 'the Athenians were obliged

47. *Athene mourning*

to abolish the democracy and in its place they handed over the government to four hundred oligarchs'. The democracy was soon restored but the time was running out and in the last years of the war it provided one of the saddest examples of its less attractive side. In 406 BC, when the people condemned to death all the generals who had been present at the sea-battle off Arginusae, they actually ignored their own laws. It seems that after the victory a storm had prevented the recovery of the shipwrecked survivors. Socrates was one of the *prytaneis* at the time:

My tribe happened to be holding the *prytaneia* at the time of the trial of the generals who had failed to pick up the survivors and the bodies of those killed after Arginusae. The Assembly proposed to try the generals all together, which was quite contrary to the law, as was widely admitted afterwards. But at the time I was the only council member who opposed the illegal move; I voted against the proposal. All the speakers threatened to prosecute me and have me arrested. The whole Assembly started shouting and screaming – but I decided that I would rather run such a risk, since I knew that law and right were both on my side, than join the rest of you in an illegal activity through fear. [Plato, *Apology* 32 ff.]

Pericles, it will be remembered, had talked not only of Athenian freedom and equality but also of their respect for the law and for each other. Somehow the last two qualities had become diminished under the strains of war. Equality, when it becomes simply a lack of judgement, and freedom, when it becomes lawlessness, are no use to anyone. Socrates was overruled; illegal their behaviour might be, but this was what the people wanted to do at that moment, and so six *strategoi*, whom they had elected only a few months before, were put to death. Two years later the war was lost, and Sparta, the victor, sailed into the Peiraeus to hand Athens over to the control of thirty tyrants.

For the time being at any rate Athens was no longer a democracy.

5
Epilogue

A few months later, a number of those exiled from Athens by the Thirty [tyrants] succeeded in defeating the tyrants and their supporters, and the democracy was restored. We cannot, unfortunately, pursue the story of Athens into the fourth century here, beyond remarking that her greatest days were over.

The story of the Athenian democracy has obvious and direct relevance to us today because the values of freedom and equality, so highly prized by the Athenians, are also prized by us. But it would be silly to pretend that either society has solved all problems, and a consideration of their failures may throw some light on the solution to some of our problems. The Old Oligarch, who is often thought of by historians as an enemy of democracy (perhaps without good reason), conveniently summarises both the essential features of the Athenian constitution and the justification of those features:

> One might argue that it is stupid to let everyone have an equal say in political matters and serve on the *Boule*, and that it would be more sensible to leave government to the more intelligent and better brought up. But really this policy of letting all men, whatever their birth or background, have their say is quite admirable; for, if only aristocrats were allowed to debate and make political decisions, it would suit *them* very nicely of course, but it would hardly suit the *demos*. As it is, anybody, however insignificant, can stand up and get what he wants for himself and others of his sort.... And it is right that the lower classes and the mass of the people should do better than the wealthy and well-born citizens under the Athenian system of government, because the people man the ships and make the city strong, not the nobles. Since this is so, it seems fair that the people should share the magistracies and speak their mind freely.
>
> [Old Oligarch 1.6 and 1.2]

This seems reasonable; but critics of democracy are not necessarily trying to turn the clock back to some kind of aristocratic society. Plato, for instance, the Athenian philosopher who had some harsh criticism to make of his city, has often (in my view) been misunderstood, and wrongly accused of wanting to keep the people in their place beneath a privileged aristocracy. This was certainly not his wish. In a famous passage he exclaims scornfully:

> In the first place aren't the citizens in a democracy free? Isn't the
> city stuffed full of liberty and freedom of speech? Isn't everybody free
> to do as he likes? There's no need to serve your city, even if you are
> well qualified to do so, if you don't feel like it; no need to abide by
> the laws if you don't like them. Make peace or make war, just as it
> suits you: do what you want, that's the cry in a democracy. All this
> variety makes it a pleasure to contemplate; and no doubt many
> regard it as a beautiful sight, just like women and children capti-
> vated by the bright pattern of a dress.   [Plato, *Republic* 557 ff.]

Plato's fear is not that the people are getting above themselves. He is worried
that people should feel that all is well, provided that everybody is free to do
as he wishes. He is worried that too heavy an emphasis on freedom may lead
to people refusing to take positive action about setting things to rights. Above
all, he is worried about the idea that a majority opinion should always make
the final decision. He believes there is a need for specialised, qualified
expertise in government – to be precise, *educated* leadership.

Democracy today is unlikely to survive if we do not take these fears
seriously. Each of us will have his own view of the unsatisfactory features of
our society: one may suggest that our society is not, in general terms, very
equal, that there is a somewhat worrying trend towards litigation, that we do
not always have a very clear idea of where popular opinion and where expert
opinion should hold sway or by what criterion such a distinction should be
made, that the freedom of the individual is increasingly threatened not only
by the state, but also by power exerted by various pressure groups, and that
some issues are still unfortunately settled by the sway of popular emotion
rather than reason, just as that first decision about Mytilene was reached so long
ago on the Pnyx.

We are still treading that delicate line between individual freedom and
state controlled fairness. We might recall Aeschylus' words when the democracy was newly born in Athens:

> Be advised by me, Athenians: avoid both the extreme of tyranny
> and the extreme of complete freedom.
>
> [Aeschylus, *Eumenides* 696 ff.]

48. *Democracy placing a wreath on the people of Athens*

Index